THE *REAL BOOK* ABOUT
FARMS

THE *REAL BOOK* ABOUT
FARMS

by

ROBERT WEST HOWARD

Illustrated by Edwin Herron

EDITED BY HELEN HOKE

Garden City Books

GARDEN CITY, NEW YORK

BY ARRANGEMENT WITH FRANKLIN WATTS, INC.

To Betsy, David and Peggy

CONTENTS

ACKNOWLEDGMENTS

The AUTHOR wishes to thank the following for their many helpful suggestions and criticisms in preparation and review of this manuscript: Dr. M. L. Wilson, Director of Extension Service, U. S. Department of Agriculture; Alfred Stefferud, editor of USDA Yearbook; Ernest L. Little, former Executive Secretary of the National Farm Chemurgic Council, and now President of Research Associates, Columbus, Ohio; Dr. Frank Cyr, Professor of Rural Education, Teachers College, Columbia University; Dr. Raymond W. Miller, Consultant to FAO of United Nations; Miss Nora Beust, U. S. Office of Education; Miss Sally Marks, Institute of Inter-American Affairs, Washington, D. C.; Mr. Lawrence Hart, K.C., Montreal, Canada.

Chapter 1

THE CAVE MAN BECOMES A FARMER

Daniel Webster, the great orator from New Hampshire, got up from his chair in the assembly room of the U. S. Senate one afternoon in 1840 and made a speech about farming. It became a very famous speech because of a remark he made in it. "When tillage begins," he said, "other arts follow. The farmers, therefore, are the founders of civilization." This sentence is still quoted frequently by farmers and at 4-H club and Future Farmer meetings.

The more you study those fourteen words Daniel Webster spoke over one hundred years ago, the more interesting they become. Civilization actually did begin with farming. When tillage (or "plowing," as we call it now) begins, schools and roads and stores and industries follow, one by one.

Even writing and arithmetic came out of farming.

The world's first farmers had to learn a method for keeping records of the crops they grew, the size of their fields, the number of their cattle, and the "swapping" they did with professional hunters and fishermen. The numbers we use today are called "Arabic." They were invented in Arabia, thousands of years ago, when the Arabs were noted all over the world for the silks, spices, sugar, cotton, melons, and other farm products they swapped between India and China on the East, and Greece, Rome, Palestine, and Carthage on the West.

Many thousands of years before that, in about 28,-000 B.C., mankind learned its first lessons about farming in this same countryside of Arabia.

The men and women who spend their lives studying ancient times are pretty much agreed that the first farms on earth were in the fertile valleys of the Euphrates and Tigris rivers. These are in the country that is now named Iraq. There, at the eastern end of the Mediterranean Sea, the climate was warm the year around; the countryside was level and free from rocks. The two rivers carried great floods of snow water and mud down from the mountains in neighboring Turkey each spring.

Consequently, the land was rich enough and the sunlight was warm enough to turn a dumping ground into the world's first farm.

And that, the archaeologists and anthropologists agree, is probably just how farming did start. The rest

The first farms were in warm river valleys of the Near East

of the world was much colder than it is today. Most of
Europe and Asia and America were buried under
glaciers of ice. Even in the warmer climate along the
Tigris and Euphrates rivers, men huddled together in
caves during the winter months. They lived on wild
game, nuts, and wild fruit. In the summer, groups of
them went on hunting and fishing expeditions along
the sunny, fertile river valleys. They camped at the
same spots, year after year. They threw the refuse from
their meals in the same place. In this refuse were the
cores of wild apples, the seeds of peaches and grapes,
and the tops from some of the roots they gnawed.

In time, one unusually bright hunter noticed that
fruit trees and new supplies of roots were growing from
the seeds in these old garbage dumps. He decided to try
out the idea of planting some seed near his home cave.

If this worked, he would have a food supply near at hand. He carried seeds back home and planted them.

But he soon learned that the root crops and young trees had to be protected from wild animals. He broke limbs from big trees, stuck them in the ground in a solid row around his crops—and invented the first fence. After that he had to invent other things, too: a place to store his roots during the winter; a way to sun-dry some of the fruit for winter use.

In time man discovered that some fields grew better crops than other fields. Also, if you had a crop growing, you couldn't wander off on a saber-toothed tiger hunt for three or four months with the rest of the fellows. You had to stay there to guard the crops, and to harvest them before the birds, animals, or your enemies got them. So the families who became interested in raising crops were forced, by the crops themselves, to settle down and stop roving.

Eventually they learned how to build houses from sun-dried bricks. These were a lot more comfortable than caves. They discovered that some of the wild animals living in the valleys—the horses, cows, dogs, and pigs—could be persuaded to live near the house if food was thrown out to them occasionally.

Then another great but unknown inventor found that a forked limb from a tree, sharpened at the fork end, would break up dirt clods and grass roots when pulled through a field. It made planting a lot easier. In time, the forked stick was given the name of "plow," which means to "pluck" or "pull up." A cow or a horse could pull a much larger plow than a man or woman could. Thus step by patient step, the farm with all its traditions was born.

Another ancient farmer noticed that a round stone could be rolled easily along the ground. If he took two round stones, drilled holes through them and ran a stick through the holes, he could build a box atop the stick. The box would carry heavy loads of farm produce. The stones would roll it along as fast as a horse, or cow, or camel could walk. Improvements were made on these rolling stones. Eventually the same kinds of circles were carved out of wood. In ancient China, farmers designed a wagon with one small wooden circle on the front end of the box and long handles out behind. They rigged a sail up at the front end. The sail helped them push the loads of produce along the mountain trails.

So the wheel, the wagon, and the wheelbarrow were invented. If we trace the word "wheel" back to its ancient beginnings, we find that it means "to cultivate."

By the time the Hittites, the Sumerians, the Babylonians, the Jews, and the Egyptians lived in this "land of milk and honey" at the east end of the Mediterranean, farming was a skilled profession. We can see, by reading the Old Testament of the Bible, how much these people knew about farming five thousand years ago.

Profession after profession developed from farming. Methods for forging bronze and iron were discovered. So miners and blacksmiths were needed to manufacture stronger plows and hoes and knives. Wheat and rye and barley had been discovered and planted in big fields along the valleys. Some of the growers were "one-crop-farmers." They had to trade wheat for the other food, clothing, and tools they needed. A new profession of "traders" was born to exchange these surplus food crops for other commodities, transport them into the villages, and swap them to the miners, blacksmiths, harness makers, tentmakers, camel drivers, carpenters, and other craftsmen who lived there.

As both farmers and villagers learned to specialize in their jobs, family names developed. Thousands of years ago some ancestor of the Ferris family, for instance, either manufactured iron tools for farmers, or was the "strong man" of his community. Because of this, his neighbors started to call him "the ferris" which really means "the man of iron." The ancestor of the Millers ground the farmer's grain into flour and livestock food. The early Shepherds herded sheep. The Browns descended from farmers with dark hair and flashing brown eyes. The Franklins were once "free-holders," or men who owned the land they farmed and so paid no tribute to the lord of the local castle. The Howards were originally "hogwards" who herded pigs through the ancient English forests.

Thus as Daniel Webster pointed out, farmers actually were the founders of civilization. The ancient cities of Babylon, Nineveh, Tyre, Rome, Athens, Jerusalem all had their beginnings in that hunter who observed fruit trees springing from the rubbish of an old camp site and developed the idea of a planted field.

Farming in the Americas began long before these Bible land cities were built. Some of these farms, along the north Pacific coast and in South America, are among the oldest in the world.

About twenty thousand years ago, it is believed, bands of adventurers from China and Siberia journeyed past the volcanoes and rocky headlands of what is now the Bering Straits to discover North and South America. We are pretty certain of the time, because of some of the things their descendants knew—and didn't know—about farming. These copper-colored, dark-haired people brought dogs into America with them. (These were the ancestors of the dogs we know today and were very different from our intelligent and devoted pets.) These early people not only used dogs for beasts of burden and for hunting, but they ate them as meat.

They did not have pigs or cows or horses. And they never did discover the wheel. Therefore, scientists have concluded that the ancestors of the American Indians left the mainland of Asia before the pig, horse, and cow were domesticated and before the wheel was invented. The dog is believed to have been the first animal tamed by man. But farmers of the Mediterranean countries had tame pigs fifteen thousand years ago. So the Indians must have journeyed over from Asia before that time.

In the forests and fields of the American continents, the Indians grew many fruits, vegetables, and grains—and raised animals—that were not known in the rest of the world. By the time Columbus landed, the Indians had discovered and tamed corn, cotton, squash, pumpkins, tomatoes, potatoes, beans, and tobacco. These new crops astonished and delighted the settlers from Europe. Indian farmers in Mexico and Peru kept large flocks of turkeys, and raised annual supplies of fish in artificial ponds.

The settlers from Europe and Africa who came to America after Columbus brought many farm animals, fruits, and plants unknown to the Indians. Most important were horses, cattle, sheep, pigs, chickens, apples, peaches, pears, wheat, oats, and many varieties of vegetables and flowers.

The Indians, being fine farmers, became as excited about horses, pigs, and cattle as the European settlers did about corn, tobacco, and turkeys. Some of the worst battles during the years of exploration were caused, according to old Spanish records, by the Indians' hunger after "roast pork." De Soto, the Spanish explorer who first ventured into Florida and across to the Mississippi Valley, told how the Indians attacked his camp time after time in order to steal some of the herd of pigs he had brought along for a food supply. Roast pig, they had discovered, was much tastier than roast dog. The Indians welcomed horses and cattle just as enthusiastically. Within a few years, the Indians of the West became excellent horsemen and cattlemen.

Except for these changes, farming remained the same for a very long time. While America was being settled, the farmer from ancient Syria would have seen few changes in the tools and methods used by the Pilgrims at Plymouth, Massachusetts and the Spanish in St. Augustine, Florida. The plow was still a forked wooden stick, faced with a thin sheet of iron. Full-grown cattle weighed only 300 pounds. No farm family, even with ten or twelve children, could plow, plant, weed and harvest more than twenty acres of land a year.

But America's soil was fabulously rich. There were fewer than 100,000 Indians from Maine to Florida. They used up very little of the land's fertility. The accumulation of minerals from millions of years of freezing and thawing and rotting produced the largest crops the world had ever seen. Some farmers, particularly in Virginia and the Carolinas, made fortunes by growing tobacco, cotton, rice, and indigo (a plant from which a blue dye is made).

Yet few actual improvements were made in farming methods during the first 150 years after the Pilgrims landed. The most noteworthy change was the inven-

"Bank barns" saved labor for the farmers

tion made by an unknown farmer in Pennsylvania. He invented a new type of barn.

This barn was two stories high, and built into a hillside that faced to the south. Thus the north end of the ground floor was buried in the hill and had "natural insulation." All the ground floor windows faced the south, so they caught the wintertime sunshine. Also, by building the barn into the bank, it was possible to drive wagons along the hillside and right into the second floor of the barn.

The Pennsylvania Dutchmen called this type of structure a "bank barn." Cattle, horses, and other livestock were housed on the sunny ground floor during the winter months. Hay and grains were stored on the second floor, and could be delivered right to the bins and haymow by the wagons. During the winter, livestock feed could be dropped down from the second floor to the first without a great deal of "lugging" by the farmer.

The Yankees in New England had never heard of this kind of a barn. Neither had the Hudson Dutchmen of New York, nor the wealthy planters in Virginia and the Carolinas. They all copied the idea, and began to build bank barns of their own.

Also, the Pennsylvania Dutchmen were very frugal. They saved some of the blood from the pigs and cattle and chickens they slaughtered and mixed it with oils and waxes in the paint they put on their barns. The animal blood was an excellent preservative for the wood. And it gave the barn a pleasing red color.

The idea of the ground floor dairy and calf pen and the second floor haymow and granary goes back to this unknown Pennsylvania Dutch inventor. So does the red color we still see on most farmers' barns—although no animal blood has been mixed in paint for a hundred years.

Aside from the bank barn, few changes occurred in American farming until the time of the Revolutionary War. Since then farm inventions have caused more changes and improvements in this way of life than took place in all the thirty thousand years before 1776. And, as in the past, each invention resulted from the work of men who devoted their lives to solving one or two problems. Some of these great inventors died in poverty and are still unknown. Others became famous and wealthy.

Benjamin Franklin, Thomas Jefferson, George Washington, and Henry Clay are among the American statesmen who were also farmers and made lasting contributions to the farm.

Franklin experimented with new crop methods on his farms in New Jersey and Pennsylvania. We owe him a vote of thanks, too, for every rhubarb pie we eat, and every broom we use. He sent back from Europe, about 1770, the first rhubarb roots and the first broomcorn seed ever seen in America.

Thomas Jefferson introduced new varieties of Spanish sheep to the United States. He spent many years on experiments with new kinds of fertilizer and plows on his Virginia farm.

George Washington, in 1796, made the first proposal that a Department of Farming be established in the Federal Government.

Henry Clay, the great orator from Kentucky, never got along too well with Daniel Webster. Their debates in the U. S. Senate are still famous. But they were in agreement on the importance of farming. Henry Clay's particular interests were in livestock. He believed that better cattle, horses, mules, and sheep should be developed for American farmers. He imported many kinds from England and Spain to his own farm in the Kentucky hills. One of these was a breed of big red beef cow that had been developed by farmers in the section of England called Herefordshire. Henry Clay named the strain, the "Hereford." The Herefords, together with the Aberdeen Angus from Scotland, became the most popular breeds of beef cattle in the West after 1880. So all the Herefords in the U.S.A. can look on Henry Clay as their "American godfather."

In 1796, a young mechanic from New Haven, Connecticut, went to South Carolina and invented a machine that separated the fuzzy green seeds in cotton bolls from the fibers. The mechanic's name was Eli Whitney. His machine was called the "cotton gin." The cotton gin made it possible for farmers to grow cotton as a cash crop all across the South, from Virginia to California.

A few years later a Virginian named Cyrus McCormick invented a machine that harvested ripe wheat and tied it into bundles. This was called a "reaper." Improvements on McCormick's machine enabled it to thresh the seeds of wheat out of the stalks and drop them into a wagon; then it wrapped the straw into bales. This was the "combine." It is the machine used today to harvest wheat and other grain crops.

In upstate New York, Jethro Wood became deeply interested in the plow. He carved models for new kinds of plows out of potatoes—because potatoes are easy to whittle—then reproduced them in iron. He finally invented a plow with a sharp point that would cut

A reaping combine does the work of many men

through the heavy grass roots of the prairies. Jethro Wood died a poor man, but his plow became the most popular type used after the invention of steel in 1863.

John Chapman, a gaunt farm preacher, trudged along the wilderness trails of Ohio and Indiana carrying bags of fruit seeds and herbs over his shoulder. He planted the seeds in forest clearings, and went back each summer or two to prune and tend the growing trees. He is remembered today as "Johnny Appleseed." Much of the fine fruit grown in the Midwest comes from descendants of the trees he planted.

A Texan named Gail Borden experimented for months in New Lebanon, New York, before he found a method to purify and can cow's milk so that it could be used to feed babies and young children on ocean voyages or during the long wagon train trips across the western prairies. He called his invention "condensed milk."

In Chicago, a young farmer from Cape Cod, Massachusetts, discovered that meat will stay fresh if stored in a box cooled by ice. He built railroad cars equipped with ice boxes. This made it possible to ship fresh meat anywhere in the U.S.A., or even to Europe. He became the owner of a great packing company. His name was Gustavus Swift.

Many other farmers worked for years to develop better varieties of sheep and cattle, horses, chickens, and pigs. Through their experiments with crossbreeding and their importation of different kinds of animals from all over the world, many new breeds were developed. In time the size of the average American cow grew from 300 to 1,200 pounds; the small shaggy Indian pony was replaced by the huge work horse; the Texas steer with long horns and tough meat gave way to the big, sweet-meated Hereford and Angus; the pig changed from a rambunctious, surly "razorback" to a fat, shiny white or red "porker" that grows tender hams, big pork chops, bacon, and yards of soft leather.

As millions of farmers from every country of Europe surged across the virgin American land, countless other experiments were made with grasses, trees, and crops. Farmers from Russia introduced the yellow "Delicious" apple and "Turkey Red" wheat. Farmers from England and Holland brought over Guernsey, Jersey and Hol-

stein milk cows. Ship captains, returning to New England from trading voyages in China and the Far East, carried home chickens that were crossbred and perfected into the Rhode Island Reds, Hampshire Reds, Plymouth Rocks and other strains we know today.

While Abraham Lincoln was president, the Federal Government gave land to help support colleges—hence called Land-Grant Colleges for "the study of agriculture and mechanics." And an Office of Agriculture was established as part of the Federal Government in Washington. Both the colleges and the federal office (which soon became the U. S. Department of Agriculture) delved into scientific experimentation on farm problems. Just as the other professions grew from the first farms in the Bible lands, the American farm soon began to develop professions previously unknown in the world. The agricultural economists, pomologists, bacteriologists, agronomists, soil conservationists, home economists, nutritionists, county agents—each developed his or her own specialty for the betterment of farms and farm families.

One small group of specialists was organized and sent out to explore all parts of the world. They were called, naturally, the "plant explorers." Their job was to discover varieties of plants and trees that could be grown profitably on American farms. In China they found the soybean, the tung tree, new kinds of plums, and new varieties of rice. They sent the seedless orange back from South America (where its ancestor had been imported from Goa, off the Indian coast). At Tangiers, in North Africa, they found a variety of orange that had a loose skin. They named it the "tangerine," and sent it off to Florida for planting.

The groves of eucalyptus trees in California today were sent in from Australia. The dates and melons growing in the irrigated deserts of California and Arizona were sent back from Africa and Persia by the plant explorers. India supplied new kinds of onions and cucumbers. South America and the distant islands of the Pacific provided new kinds of sugar cane, peanuts, sweet potatoes, and yams.

So the crops of America changed. Farmers became more and more skilled because of new knowledge of soil and water, minerals and sunshine discovered by the college and governmental specialists. But the greatest farm changes of all came after 1890 when Henry Ford and others invented a vehicle that could be fueled with gasoline. Then for the first time in the thirty thousand years of his history, the farmer had a huge reserve of mobile power at his command.

Railroad trains can run only on rails. Steamboats are

helpless out of the water. But a gasoline engine, hitched to that wheel that a nameless farmer discovered thousands of years ago, can go anywhere—up muddy roads, across lots and even (with the right kind of wheels) through swamps and over stone walls.

Gasoline engines, attached to wagons, became the trucks that carry farm crops from barnyard to city in a few minutes or hours. Gasoline engines, with very small wheels before and very large wheels behind, became the tractors that pull plows, cultivators, harrows, combines, corn pickers, and other farm tools across the fields.

The gasoline engine, as the power center of automobiles, trucks, and tractors, created the greatest revolution in the history of farming. This year, American farmers own more than 3,500,000 tractors and 3,000,000 trucks. Macadam and concrete highways have replaced the dirt roads. Electric power lines and telephone wires pace them across the countryside, from farm to farm.

That is the principal reason why all the foods and fibers and leathers and oils needed by America can be produced today by just one-fifteenth of the families who live in America—that is, every farm family produces enough food, clothing, and all of the other things needed for fifteen other families.

In spite of all of this progress, all farmers know that this is not the end of their history. The challenges and explorations ahead are just as exciting and as promising as any that have been made up to date. There is a vast "unknown land" of invention and discovery still ahead. Leadership in this exploration will come from the farmers of 1970 and 1980. Perhaps you will be one of them.

Chapter 2

FISH FARMS AND MINK RANCHES

A CAREER in farming may lead to a life on any one of a great many different kinds of farms. Because the climate, the soil, and many other factors make some things grow in one place that wouldn't grow at all in another.

We don't expect to see monkeys running around with the pigs on an Illinois farm, or coconut trees growing wild in Minnesota. It would be just as strange to boys and girls in Central America and Africa to see a skunk waddle around the back yard with the pet monkeys or to have a beautiful red maple tree growing wild among their banana plants. The monkey's and the coconut's home in Central America and Africa, like the red maple's and skunk's home in the north country, was decided thousands of years ago by the sun and the soil in these places.

28

Monkeys and coconuts both need warm weather the year around. So they stay near the equator, where there is enough sunlight all twelve months of the year to keep them warm. Skunks, however, grow a heavy coat of fur for the winter months, then shed it during the spring and summer. (That is why fur buyers pay more for winter pelts than they do for summer pelts.) A skunk dressed in his long winter coat would be most uncomfortable, and probably get sick and die, near the equator.

The red maple tree has adjusted to the north country's summer-and-winter climate, too. It reverses the skunk's system, in a way. The red maple puts out leaves in spring and summer. The leaves provide shade for the roots of the tree and keep the sun from drying them out. In winter, the red maple sheds its leaves, the circulation of sap through its trunk and branches slows down, and the trunk and roots go to sleep, very much as we do when we relax.

Both the earth and the sun are whirling through space. Our part of the earth, the Northern Hemisphere, comes closest to the sun in summertime. Then the days are longer, and more warmth from the burning sun penetrates the ground.

Seeds sprout into plants and produce flowers and fruit only when the temperature of the soil and the surrounding air is above 38° Fahrenheit. Our summertime weather stays well above 38 degrees and that is why summertime is growing time on the farm.

The sun creates the same kind of growing urge in animals. Hens hatch their broods of baby chicks in springtime. Baby pigs born in the spring are healthier and grow faster than those born at other seasons of the year. Cows and horses, rabbits and geese, woodchucks and snakes all follow the same rule—handed down by the sun.

Growing seasons come at different times, of course, in different parts of the world. Farms south of the equator, in South America, South Africa, and Australia have their summertime during December, January, and February. They have their winter, or rainy season, while we in the Northern Hemisphere are having our summer. The equator gets more sunlight and more warmth than land either far north or far south. Farms in Virginia and Alabama and Texas are closer to the equator than farms in Maine and Ohio and Montana. Therefore, they have long summers and short winters or, as farmers say, they have a longer "growing season." Since some crops take longer to grow than others, you will naturally find them growing in the South.

In addition to many different kinds of foods, farms supply the raw materials for many of the things we use every day, such as clothing, medicine, footballs, furniture, and plastics. Because of this, there are hundreds of different kinds of farms. Some of them aren't even on land. Some are called "ranches" and some are called "plantations." Let's take a quick look at a few of the unusual ones that are not in the least like "old MacDonald's" farm full of quacking ducks and clucking chickens.

Oyster Farms

Along the coast of Long Island, near New York City, and off the coast of Louisiana, in the Gulf of Mexico, are large farms that grow oysters. They are as carefully cared for as land farms.

The shallow water where oysters are to be grown is dredged and cleared of refuse each May. In June, shells for the baby oyster "set" to grow on are strewn over the same undersea field. These shells protect the oysters from their enemies the starfish, drumfish, conch, mussels, and leech. The average female oyster lays 16,000,-000 eggs. These hatch in July. No harvesting is done during the planting and growing time, which is why oysters aren't sold between April and September.

A baby oyster is one three-thousandth of an inch long. It has a tail and swims freely during the first two weeks of life. After that it "sets"—attaches itself firmly to a rock or shell on the sea bottom—loses its tail and begins to grow a shell of its own. It is one seventy-fifth of an inch long when this happens.

Two or three months later, when the oysters are dredged up and carried off to market, they are still gripping firmly to the pieces of shell they "set" on. The discarded shells, after the oysters have been removed, are either ground up and sold to land farmers as chicken feed, or thrown back into the ocean for a new generation of "set."

Fish Farms

There are fish farms, too. The farmers of France have made fish an important part of their production ever since the Middle Ages. They build dirt walls, or dikes, around grain fields in the late fall, after harvest time. Then they flood the fields with water and plant this new pond with baby fish.

Within a year, the fish are large enough to eat. A pond of this type will grow an average of 500 pounds of fish per acre each year. After two or three years, the dike is broken. The field dries out. The dead fish and refuse remaining are plowed into the land as fertilizer.

Thus through a shift from land to water and back to land again, these French farmers not only make their land richer and healthier but keep it busy growing food all the time.

Bee Farms

Beekeeping is a kind of farming known to be at least six thousand years old. It was as well known in Egypt at the time of the Pharaohs as it is today—and as important. Bees manufacture honey that is flavored by the flowers they eat. The chewy wax they spin around each

Beekeeping is an ancient and unusual kind of farming

drop of honey is called the "comb." It is used in medicines, furniture polishes, as patterns for industrial machines, and as a kind of "grease" on ammunition for guns. In gathering the nectar and pollen from flowers, to make their wax and honey, the bees do a very important transfer job known as "pollination."

All flowering plants, including grasses and trees, produce their seed through a complicated process that takes place inside the flower. Seeds will not begin to grow until the grains of yellow dust growing on small stalks inside the flower attach themselves to the stigma, or central stalk, inside the flower. The yellow dust is made up of sperm cells and is called "pollen."

The bee dives headlong into the open flower to gather its sweet sap, called "nectar." His furry hind legs collect some of the pollen. If a grain of this pollen

Fur farming needs wild surroundings

brushes off the bee's leg on to the stigma of that flower or another one, the flower is "fertilized." It starts to produce its seed. This whole process is called pollination.

Bee farms, then, should be located near farms that grow fruit, or flowering plants such as clover, buckwheat, alfalfa, and sage. In our Far West, beekeepers place the hives containing their colonies of bees on big trucks. They move them from farm to farm during the growing season. The farmers pay the beekeepers for the pollinization work the bees do on their trees and plants. During those weeks, the truck on which the hives are stored is actually a bee farm.

Fur Farms

Fur farming requires quiet country and a very careful imitation of the surroundings in which the animals

34

live when wild. Mink and beaver and raccoon raised in captivity have to be supplied with the kinds of fresh running water their ancestors lived in and near for thousands of years. Foxes must be placed in shadowy pens they can't dig out of and must be fed lots of gamey raw meat.

Specialty Crops

Some farms grow rabbits, herbs, water cress, peppermint, cranberries, tung trees, castor beans, blueberries, and other plants and animals as "specialty crops." Each plant and each animal has its own methods of growth. Each one requires special treatment.

Cranberries will grow only on low, marshy land, hugging the salt water of the oceans. Blueberries grow best on rocky, dry ground that is burned every two or three years. Tung trees, whose nut-like fruit contains the sticky, yellow ingredient of house paint called tung oil, flourish on the desolate, hot sand dunes along the Gulf coast of Mississippi, Alabama, and Florida.

But these specialty crops do not take up much of our American farmland. Only 40,000 acres of land (out of our 1,200,000,000 acres) are needed to grow the 1,-000,000 pounds of peppermint we use each year to flavor chewing gum, candy, toothpaste, toothache drops, and other drugstore products. The cranberry farms of the U.S.A., despite the popularity of the fruit at Thanksgiving and Christmas, occupy a total of only

30,000 acres. The state of Maine, with America's largest blueberry crop, has only about 150,000 acres of these fruit bushes.

So, as big as these farm plots for growing specialty crops may seem, they are a very tiny fraction of all the land used by farms in the United States. Most farms are producing the staple food and clothing that the country uses—meat and vegetables, wool and cotton. It takes many different kinds of land and many different kinds of farming to produce the staggering quantities of these things that we need. And it takes all of the latest inventions in science and machinery—the modern farmer is not only a tiller of the soil, he is a master mechanic, a scientist, and a businessman all in one!

Chapter 3
TEAMWORK MAKES THE FARM

THE TERM of measurement commonly used for land on American farms is "acre." The square measure table in arithmetic books says that an acre is 4,840 square yards. A simple way to say it, these days, is that if you walk 210 feet, or 70 long steps, you have covered one side of a square acre.

A farm, according to the definition of the U. S. Bureau of the Census, can be any area of land from two and a half acres on up that is used to grow crops or livestock "for profit." American farms, which are very large in the opinion of farmers of Europe and Asia, range in size from two and a half to one hundred thousand acres, and in Japan and China, most rural families must make their living on farms of only one or two acres.

Outside of the specialty farms, there are two kinds of farms that produce the bulk of our produce. The first

A variety of crops and animals grow on diversified farms

and most numerous is called a "diversified" or "family farm." Most of the farms on the Atlantic seaboard as far west as Chicago are in this class. They were given that name because each farm is operated by one family. Its teamwork is so organized that it grows several kinds of crops and animals. Thus it "diversifies" the goods it has to sell on the public market.

A diversified family farm in New York State, such as the John Ferris place which we will talk about later, might have thirty-five dairy cows, fifty pigs, twenty sheep, a flock of two hundred chickens, ten acres of apple trees, twenty acres of potatoes, ten acres of broccoli, twenty-five acres of "wood lot" or forest, twenty acres of corn, ten acres of clover, and fifty acres of pasture land.

The milk given by the thirty-five cows each day is

sold to a dairy company in a near-by village, then shipped by tank car or truck to New York City. There it is either sold as fresh milk, mixed in with ice cream, churned into butter, or curdled and pressed into any one of twenty-five varieties of cheese. It is possible to extract a kind of curd called "casein" from this milk. Casein, in liquid form, gives the shiny, slick feeling and appearance to the paper used in magazines. It can also be spun into fibers that make excellent "felt" hats and "woolly" neckties.

The fifty pigs on the farm will, of course, be sold in the market during the fall and become pork chops, bacon, ham, sausage, spareribs, smoked tenderloins, and headcheese. The pigs' skins will be tanned and turned into gloves, brief cases and footballs. Tiny glands in the pigs' necks will be condensed and purified into a drug called ACTH which has already proven to be a miraculous medicine for treating burns.

The sheep eventually become wool, lamb chops, and an oil named "lanolin" (which is the "slickum" in most hair tonics as well as the base for shaving creams and many ointments).

The chickens, after laying an average of 160 eggs apiece each year, wind up in somebody's refrigerator. Their feathers go off to a mattress factory, or perhaps disappear into a vat of dye and eventually become the fluffy decorations on a new hat. Incidentally, you may be wearing clothing made from chicken feathers some

One-crop farms grow only one kind of product

day! A process has been discovered which dissolves the feathers into a heavy syrup, squirts it out through tubes that turn the syrup into a thread. Fabrics spun from this thread look and feel like wool, wash easily and have no odor. Feathers from thirty-eight chickens will produce enough of this fabric for a man's suit.

Apples, potatoes, and broccoli are all sold to a city produce market. The clover and corn go into the barns to feed the cows and other livestock during the winter. Every few years, the largest trees in the wood lot are cut down, and turned into firewood or lumber.

The second type of American farm is called simply a "one-crop farm." Most of the ranches of the West and the plantations of the South are of this kind. When the invention of the cotton gin by Eli Whitney in 1796 enabled owners of southern plantations to make large

A western cattle ranch is a one-crop farm

profits by growing short-staple or "upland" cotton, millions of acres were quickly planted with this crop. No other crops were grown on these plantations.

The same sort of system is being followed on western prairie lands today, where wheat is the most profitable crop the land will produce.

The cattle and sheep ranches of the Far West also are one-crop farms. As in all types of farming, the sun determines what the land is going to be best for—and ranch land usually is useful only for grazing beef cattle, sheep, and horses.

Fruit farms are a very particular type of one-crop farm, especially in Florida, Texas, Arizona, and California where most of our oranges, grapefruit, lemons, limes, and other citrus fruits grow. Modern fruit farming, because of the many inventions made for refrigerating, canning, and quick-freezing the fruit, has become as complicated a year-round job as diversified farming.

In choosing what crops to plant, the farmer has to consider the costs and income involved as well as the kind of soil and climate he has to deal with. For farming is a business, and so the farmer has to figure his "turn-over" in investment and return just as in any other business. For instance, vegetables and grain crops are planned, planted, and harvested in one year. Chickens and pigs are a one-year investment; dairy and beef cattle are a three- or four-year investment—that is, it takes three or four years before cattle can be raised and sold to get the money back that the farmer has spent on them. A fruit orchard is a much longer investment—it takes ten to twenty-five years before young fruit trees can begin to pay for themselves.

Maybe this is one reason why only two and a half million of the forty-six million American families are "farm families!" It is true that an additional three and a half million families live on farms and grow some of their own foodstuff and perhaps a few specialty crops to sell—but they earn their livelihood from jobs or professions in near-by cities.

However, the two and a half million farm families who work at farming full time produce enough of everything for the forty-six million families—and some over to sell to other countries. They can do this only because of modern tractors and combines and other machines—including the helicopter—and because of the close teamwork man has developed between sun and soil, man and machine. In fact, farming is something like a football game in which the sun is the coach and the farmer is the quarterback who calls the signals and decides the plays. His linemen are animals, plants, and speedy machines. The soil itself is his sturdy, dependable center. Forests, water, and fertilizers are his other backs. And off on the sidelines as grand director of strategy—sending in warmth or cold, rain or drought—sits the mighty coach of the team, the sun.

In our part of the world, every farm game takes a full year to play. But, as in football, this real life game has four quarters. They are called spring, summer, fall, and winter. Each one is as important to the team's success as the others. And the farm has its cheerleaders and water boys and doctors, too, in the birds, bees, snakes, angleworms, and soil microbes which all help in their special ways.

In this farm "game," the machine was named as one of the linemen because it is almost as important on a farm today as the plants and animals. Back in 1900, for instance, a team of two horses could plow two acres of land in a ten-hour day. Today the average "tractor" plows twenty-eight acres in the same length of time. And a skilled workman will pick the ripe ears from one and a half acres of corn in a ten-hour day: a machine, called a "mechanical picker," designed for the same task, will harvest twelve acres per day. It takes a man nine minutes to milk a cow by hand, but by machine many cows can be milked at one time.

In the cotton fields and citrus groves of the South, the horizon-sweeping wheat ranches of the West, the corn and soybean farms of the prairie, the fruit orchards and dairy farms of Wisconsin, and on the Atlantic coast the same great change has taken place in farming methods during the past forty years. It has been the most exciting era in all the thirty thousand years since farming began. And it is still going on. More and more machinery is being invented for the farmer's use. More and more discoveries are being made about the mysterious powers of sunlight and soil and water, the growing habits of seeds, and all the other players on the farm team.

These inventions and discoveries have made it possible for American farmers to produce a vast avalanche of food and raw materials each year, totaling billions of tons. If we figure this out in terms that are easier to understand, we will find that enough is produced each year for every American to have the following: one-fourth the milk supply of a dairy cow; the meat from one-fifth of a beef cow, one-half of a pig, plus some lamb and poultry; the eggs from two hens; the vegetables from one-tenth of an acre of garden; the fruit from one-quarter of an acre of orchard; the honey from two-thirds of a hive of bees (or one-hundredth of an acre of sugar cane).

Getting back to how it is that our comparatively few farmers are able to accomplish all this, we will see that it takes more than a farmer and a lot of machines to run a farm. It takes a lot of people. And so most farmers have large families, with four or five and sometimes ten children. And generally the children are all on the team. Even with school and 4-H clubs and plenty of fun, farm children have an important part to play in the big game.

A farm family lives in a big house near the center of the farm. Most farm homes are built of wood and painted white, with black or green shutters on the windows. Some of them, particularly in the Midwest and along the Pacific coast, are very modern and have radiant heating built into their floors. More than three-fourths of all farm homes in America now have electric lights, radio sets, bathrooms, running water, and deep-freeze units.

Although these homes may seem large in comparison with a city apartment, they are tiny by comparison to the huge barns that stand behind them. Dairy cows, calves, horses, and mules have their winter quarters on the ground floor of these barns. The top floors are used to store hay and grain. Most farms now have a separate building near by where tractors, trucks, and the big farm machinery are garaged. The pigs have separate little buildings in a near-by field. The chickens have their own long, low "poultry house," too, with large windows, electric lights, and stoves for winter heating.

The farmer's house is close to the barn and other buildings because, as we said before, the farmer is very much like the quarterback on a football team. He must be on his toes the year round to watch the condition of his crops, to fight against invasions of bugs, to feed his animals and, most important of all, to keep an eye on the real coach of farming's game—the sun.

As a matter of fact, a diversified farm has several games going on at the same time—because there are more things doing on this type than on a one-crop farm. Diversified farmers must know the rules for chickens as well as for trees. There are baby calves to feed, gardens to tend, corn crops to grow, apple trees to prune and spray and harvest, cows to milk, hay to cut. So there's much to be learned about many kinds of farming and the way of life "down on the farm" by watching a diversified farm operate during its four quarters. Let's take a close look at a typical one and see what it is like to play a real life game on a family farm team.

Chapter 4

A FARM FAMILY

DAVID PUTNAM, the county agent at Middleburg, says that John Ferris down in the Kerhonkson River country has a good diversified farm. "Real nice family," he drawls, "and theirs is about as substantial a family farm as you'll find in the country."

Mr. Putnam is the man employed by the U. S. Department of Agriculture and the state government to help all the farmers in the county. He gives free advice on the kinds of crops to plant, the sprays to be used in fighting different kinds of pests, and the latest scientific and machine inventions for farm use. There are over three thousand men like David Putnam in the U. S. A. —one for every county that has farms in it. That is why they are called county agents.

When they were young, David Putnam and John Ferris went to school together at the New York State

College of Agriculture in Cornell University at Ithaca. They studied for four years there. As students they went on field trips together to inspect the big milk pasteurizing plants in New York City, the grain elevators and flour mills in Buffalo, the produce markets in Syracuse and Albany. They stayed up all night, too, working over sick cows in the barns on the hilltop behind the college. A professor watched everything they did and graded them according to the way they examined each cow, diagnosed her illness, prescribed medicine for her, and held her mouth open to pour the medicines in.

At graduation time, David and John were each offered jobs in the Extension Service, the branch of the U. S. Department of Agriculture that supervises the work of the county agents. David Putnam took the offer. But John Ferris shook his head and grinned and said, "No, thanks. I'm heading back to the family place. There's a girl waiting there for me, too."

Grandfather and Grandmother Ferris had decided, the week John announced he was going to marry Margaret, that they would turn the farm, "lock, stock, and barrel," over to him. But it wasn't a gift. Grandpa Ferris doesn't believe in "bringing youngsters up on a silver tray. It does 'em good to make them work for things. Hothouse plants can't stand up against a frost. Youngsters are the same way."

The lawyers and assessors were called in. They put a "fair price" on the buildings and the land. The president of the bank in Middleburg had a long talk with John. A business arrangement was made between the bank and John whereby John could make a "down payment" to his parents. This made it possible for them to buy a cottage in Middleburg. They bought a small one so that Grandma wouldn't have too much housework to do. Behind the cottage was a small garden, just large enough to give Grandpa, as he expresses it, "some exercise for my green thumb." John is paying them the rest of the money for the farm out of his profits each year. This, too, is done through the bank on an arrangement called a Family Trust Mortgage. This money, combined with their savings, keeps them very comfortably in their old age. And then, they have their own home, too. The two families never "get underfoot" with one another as families sometimes used to when it was the custom for several generations to live in the same house. This is one of the new, wise arrangements being made between farmers and their grown children these days. People live a lot longer than they did fifty years ago. Now many farmers who retire at sixty may live to be eighty-five or ninety.

Betsy Ferris was born the year after John and Margaret were married. David Putnam sent 100 fuzzy Hampshire Red chicks out to the Ferris farm with a little note that said, "Put the profits from these deep down in the sock. She'll want to go to college someday."

Two years later, Betsy woke up one morning, and heard a noise like a kitten with its tail caught in the door. She tiptoed into the big front bedroom where old Dr. Waters and her father stood. They were grinning down at the new baby brother in her mother's arms. Of course he was named "David John" and got a silver spoon and a feeding dish with initials on it from his big, grinning godfather. There was a note with these presents. It said, "This is just a stopgap. He'll have to wait nine years for the real present."

Betsy and David grew up and graduated from mashed carrots to raw carrots. Their legs grew as long as a colt's. John Ferris said they must be hollow legs, judging from all the food they could "put away" at one meal.

It didn't seem very long, really—what with all the things there are to do on the farm—until a big, yellow bus pulled up in front of the house one September morning. The thirty kids inside the bus stared curiously out the windows while Betsy ran down the walk with her pigtails flying, then clambered aboard for her first day of school. She was starting third grade when David joined the "Bus Sixteen Crowd." That was only three years ago, the fall before baby Peggy tumbled into the world whooping like a little Indian—and just as red.

That's how there got to be five Ferrises living in the white house beside Kerhonkson Creek, with its big red barns looming up across the macadam highway, and the apple orchard curving up the hillside to a forest of hickory and maple trees.

It is only a twenty-minute ride from the Ferris place to Middleburg on the yellow school bus. Children from miles away ride to Middleburg Central School even though, in the wintertime, the busses have to wear steel plows on their front bumpers to push through the snowdrifts. John Ferris, and Grandfather before him, used to walk down the road a mile to the little red schoolhouse at the intersection. The roads were narrow dirt lanes in those days. The school had one teacher for all eight grades. Grandfather claims that one of the teachers he had there was only sixteen years old, and that five of the boys in the school were taller and older than she was. They didn't learn much that year, he said. But then schools were open only three or four months a year, during the winter when there wasn't much work to be done around the farms. In those days, every child in the family who was more than five years old had to help with farm work from April until the end of harvesttime in November.

The Middleburg Central School was built in 1940. It is prettier and shinier and more fun than most city schools. The building itself is nearly a block long, but only two stories high. It is on the edge of town and well back from the highway. A long circular drive winds across the lawns up to the front steps. The school busses have their garage at the rear.

All the classrooms have high, wide windows that let in plenty of sunlight. There are four sets of stairways so that students can get from one floor to the other without having to make long walks up and down the corridors. The library, at the center of the second floor, has thousands of books and magazines on display. Parents use it, as well as the students. It stays open all day Saturday so that farm families, in town for their week-end shopping, can come over to "browse."

The school serves the whole community. In it the "Grange," the "Farm Bureau," the "Soil Conservation Service," the "Kerhonkson Valley Farmers Co-operative," and some of the other farmer organizations hold their meetings and special parties and dinners. It is open, too, four nights a week for classes for adults in welding, soil testing, machinery repair, and some of the other things John Ferris and his neighbor farmers must study in order to "keep up with the world."

Every Saturday morning John drives in to the school to teach a class of thirty-five veterans of World War II about agriculture. The Veterans Administration in Washington pays his salary and buys all the books and class equipment. All these veterans either own farms or are saving money to shift from their present jobs to farming as soon as they have enough for the down payment on some cropland.

John Ferris and the other farmers in Kerhonkson Valley are glad to see more and more young men take an interest in farming and in the land's welfare. "Farming needs more smart youngsters in it," John says. "The smarter they are, the better it will be for everybody—for us as well as for the people who live in the city."

John and his veterans meet in a classroom most of the time. But when there are moving pictures to be shown about special farming processes, or slow-motion "shots" of the way plants grow, they go over to the school's auditorium. This is just like a city theater, with a movie projection booth, tiers of seats with plastic covers, long drapes at the windows, fire exits, an orchestra pit, and a wide stage. Whenever important speakers come to Middleburg, they talk from this stage. The town has a summer theater, too, that puts on plays here during July and August. And the Middleburg Concert Orchestra gives a series of concerts here on Saturday nights during the wintertime. The musicians in the orchestra are farmers, drugstore proprietors, the ticket agent at the bus depot, two ministers, three lawyers, the chief of police, and several housewives. Harry Malone, the traffic cop at the intersection of Main and School streets, is the orchestra's conductor. ("And why not!" Grandpa Ferris said. "He's so used to waggling his arms at automobiles, it comes natural to him.")

The school building, with its classrooms for both the

grade and high school pupils, its meeting rooms, library, auditorium, and gymnasium, occupies only a small part of the school "plot." Modern rural schools, the educational experts say, should have ten acres of land, or as much as two and a half city blocks, at least. The Middleburg Central School has fifteen acres, including a football field, a baseball diamond, a swimming pool, a tennis court, a large playground with slides, swings and a driving track where anybody in the school district can take lessons and learn how to drive an automobile or a tractor. Over beyond that, there is the croquet lawn, and a bowling green for retired farmers and other gentlemen in the village who are Grandpa Ferris' age and much older.

Finally, there are five acres of woodland, with picnic tables and wild flowers and stone fireplaces. Each class in the school is official caretaker for a section of this woodland. The students of the class police it to pick up trash and papers. They tend the flowers, rake the leaves and, from time to time, plant new trees in their section. The upper grades and high school use the woodland for field studies in botany, geology, chemistry, and physics.

Central School is important not only in the lives of Betsy, David, and Peggy, but also in the lives of John and Margaret. In recent years these big new schools in farming areas all over the country have become combinations of schoolhouse and community center and clubhouse. Adults as well as children come there to add to their education. Sometimes, on school day evenings or Saturday afternoons, a demonstrator from a machine manufacturing plant will go out to the driving track with his new "line" of tractors, plows, disks, harrows, milking machines, manure spreaders, and trailers. He will line them up there for all the farmers to see, then run each machine through its paces.

The cafeteria and school kitchen are used by farmers' wives and daughters. Special lectures on cooking and housekeeping are given there by experts from the State College of Home Economics, or by manufacturers' representatives. During the summer months, although school is "out," the director of the cafeteria and the school's dietitian stay right on their jobs. They help all the women of the district with special problems in canning, preserving, and deep-freezing the food supplies for each family's use during the winter months.

So, as Betsy and David and Peggy grow up, schools are becoming more and more important to everyone in the community. People make more friends when all the people from half a county get together in one school. In the old days, only a dozen families along a three-mile stretch of road sent children to the little one-room district schools.

Changes have been just as great on the Ferris farm too. The Ferrises used to be noted for the fine horses they kept. Great-grandpa Ferris always drove a pair of high-stepping "spotted grays" to church on Sunday morning, and into town for shopping on Saturday afternoons. Four other teams of big, burly Belgian draft horses lived in the stalls on the ground floor of the barn. Today, John keeps a mare for Margaret to ride, and a Shetland pony for the children. All the other "horsepower" work on the farm is done by tractors, trucks and a jeep.

The fine old crystal and brass oil lamps disappeared years ago, too (except for the two or three that Margaret keeps trimmed and ready for use in case thunderstorms or blizzards break down the electric power lines).

The radio sets in the living room and bedrooms have better reception than city radio sets. John even had a radio put in the cow barn. It's a proved fact that radio music makes cows more relaxed, and keeps them from twisting and kicking and swishing their heavy tails so much while they are being milked. The pictures on the television set, too, are clear and steady because of the lack of interference in the open countryside.

Another great invention that has come into the Ferris home during Betsy and David's lifetime is the deep freeze. If you have one of these square white electric boxes in your home, you may think of it as just a very nice place to keep popsicles and ice cream and candy bars. But for many of the families on American farms, it has meant a change in eating habits.

Stories about life down on the farm "in the good old days" usually describe the huge dinners served at harvesttime, Thanksgiving, and Christmas. The menus for these meals included a great many kinds of pickles, relishes, salted meats, smoked meats, and "canned stuff."

The reason for this was very simple. Farmers had no way to keep fresh foods. They lived, from harvest to harvest, on foods that could be preserved with salt, or vinegar, or smoke, plus the few kinds of vegetables and fruit that could be stored away in barrels or in dry sand "pits." Processes of canning goods in the farm kitchens weren't perfected until a few years ago. When John Ferris was a boy, pressure cookers were unknown. Bacteria and mold destroyed much of the farm wife's tempting supply of canned goods.

The invention of the deep freeze changed all this. Now fruits and vegetables can be processed, wrapped and "put down" in the freezer chest the same day they are harvested. Pork, lamb, beef, and poultry can be frozen "fresh" the year around. Such wonderful farm delicacies as fresh huckleberry pie, strawberry shortcake, blackberry cake, brown Betty, and deep-dish peach pie can be prepared in the summer when the fruits are at their peaks of perfection, then wrapped in cellophane and quick-frozen until the following January or March.

The same invention makes it possible for farmers

in all sections of the country to swap with farmers from other sections, through their co-operatives. Now, each fall, John Ferris sends barrels of his fine Northern Spy and McIntosh apples to farmers in Alabama, Florida, and Georgia. The Alabama farmer swaps back with a barrel of his fine yams each fall; the Florida farmer sends several cases of frozen orange and grapefruit juice from his groves; the Georgia farmer swaps off with big rattlesnake watermelons in July, fresh peaches in August, and a ten-pound sack of pecans just before Christmas.

These are just a few of the changes that have occurred on the Ferris place since John took over. But that doesn't mean that Grandma and Grandpa Ferris are unhappy about the changes or that they are "old fashioned," or "backward." They are just as happy about the changes as are John, Margaret, Betsy, David, and Peggy. The times have changed the people.

At school you may still sing "Old MacDonald Had a Farm," or pitch in and help "Hitch old Dobbin to the shay." They are just as much a part of history as George Washington and Abraham Lincoln. For the farm world that Betsy and David and Peggy are growing up in is a far different world than the one Grandma and Grandpa Ferris grew up in. This is true even though they live in the same fine white house beside the same creek, looking at the same sky—and are fighting and planning through the same four seasons, year after year.

I thought I should tell you about all of this before spring comes up over the hill and David puts his skates away and starts to ask Margaret, "Mom, where's my swimming suit?"

Chapter 5
PLANTING TIME

I F IT SNOWS, the outdoor air is freezing cold. The tiny
column of liquid inside the thermometer stands at
32 degrees, or lower.

If it rains, the outdoor air is warmer. The liquid in
the thermometer goes above 32 degrees.

When the thermometers rise above 32 degrees, and
stay there most of the day, the winter frost starts to melt
out of the ground. The ice on the ponds and creeks
turns the soil to mud. Water flows across the roadways
and down the fields toward the creeks, and on into the
rivers, the reservoirs, and finally roars on to the oceans.

When this happens, and all out of doors smells like
cinnamon toast, when the crows begin to fly in circles
over last year's cornfield, crying a monotonous "caw,
caw, caw," when bullfrogs peer out from their winter
quarters along the creek bank and demand a "buttered

bun, buttered bun, buttered bun" each sundown, then spring is on the way. And this, rather than January 1, is the beginning of the farm's year.

Then David, when the school bus drops him at the front gate, quickly changes from corduroys into blue levis and rubber boots. Betsy puts on overalls, too. They drink the glasses of milk that Mother has put out on the kitchen table for them and race off toward the barns.

David splashes through the mud, out past the silo and the truck shed and up the concrete ramp to the second floor of the big barn. Last fall's hay and straw is stacked in square bales almost to the roof on the left side of this floor. On the right side is a square room that has concrete walls and floor to keep out rats, squirrels, and mice. Sacks of grain and other seeds are stored here. Most of this seed was saved from last year's harvest. The rest was purchased from other farmers and seed dealers, during January and February. With spring coming on, each bag of seed must be inspected and prepared for planting time. John and David go carefully through each sack, handful by handful, to pick out dirt, chaff, and the seeds of weeds that were accidentally mixed in during the rush and bustle of harvesttime. David can identify seeds of each kind at a glance. Most weed seeds are dark brown or black. They have a villainous look about them.

During January, while John planned his crops for

the year, David had drawn a "plotting map" of the farm and pinned it up on the seed room door. He had colored the forest wood lot a dark green. The fields to be planted to corn were a bright yellow. The wheat and rye fields were purple and blue. The apple orchard was dark red. David shaded the big field where broccoli was to be planted a light brown.

John has decided to spread plenty of nitrogen and lime fertilizer on the corn and broccoli fields this spring. Clover seed will be planted on part of the pasture land but it will not bloom until next spring. John looked over at David and grinned as he thought, "There'll be more need for it, then." David Putnam, the county agent, had called John a few mornings ago. "Little David's birthday is coming in June," he had said to John. "He will be nine years old then. And—well, there will be need for a bigger clover crop next year!"

David wondered what John was grinning about. He didn't ask though. When Daddy smiled that way, there was usually a surprise of some sort afoot—and you couldn't pull the secret out of him with two tractors. Anyway, the surprise was always fun when it happened.

David sat down on the bench beside John and grinned back. "Gee, Pop," he said, "you've done a dozen bags today. You know what? Betsy says she saw a robin right by the creek bridge on the way to school this morning. D'you suppose it was? Gee whiz, we

Betsy is becoming an expert chicken farmer

got to get a move on, huh?" He leaned forward, pulled up a handful of seed and went to work.

Meanwhile, Betsy had gone down past the barn to the chicken house. Betsy is becoming an expert chicken farmer, although she is only eleven years old. The 100 chicks Big David gave her when she was born have increased to a flock of 200. Of these fifty are "yearlings," or one-year-olds. They are mated with the five big roosters. After the hens and roosters have mated, the hens lay eggs that are "fertile." Fertile eggs will produce chicks. The other 145 young hens, called "pullets," lay the eggs that are packed in crates and shipped off to storekeepers in New York City.

When Betsy arrived, Mother and little Peggy were standing beside a large machine just inside the chicken house. It looked like a bureau, made of steel and .

63

painted brown. There were small glass windows in its front, and electric switches and meters along one side. Behind the windows were rows of slender drawers. This is an electric incubator. It takes the place of the mother hens in hatching baby chicks from the fertile eggs.

Peggy stood close to a market basket filled with clean eggs. She picked up one egg at a time and handed it to Mother. Mother placed the egg, end up, in the rack inside one of the incubator trays. Peggy turned, as Betsy opened the door. She held an egg toward her and laughed. "Lots of baby chicks, for Easter time," she said and nodded her head so vigorously that her long curls tumbled across her eyes.

"Don't drop the egg," Betsy squealed, and lifted it out of Peggy's hand. "Incubators can't make chicks out of scrambled eggs!"

Quickly they filled the rest of the tray with eggs and pushed it back into the incubator. Then they pulled out the trays already filled with eggs and turned each egg upside down.

The electric heater keeps the inside of the incubator at about 100 degrees (that's about as warm as a "blistering hot" day in July). The eggs on the trays are not disturbed during the first three days. Then from the fourth to the eighteenth day, each egg must be turned upside down daily.

On the nineteenth day, if all goes well, the eggs start

to rock and bounce in the trays. A yellow beak pecks through the shell, followed by coal black eyes and a fuzzy, wet head. On the twenty-first day, wobbly-legged baby chicks stand cheeping beside the broken shells. Mother, Betsy, and Peggy carefully lift them out and carry them back to the mother hens. The hens and chicks are kept in small pens in a corner of the warm chicken house. Chicks aren't fed anything for the first thirty-six hours. After that, they receive small quantities of "chick feed" which contains sour milk, finely ground grains, and scraps of ground sea shells. They drink lots of fresh water, too.

Day by day, as the sun shines longer and warmer on the Kerhonkson Creek countryside, the big game gets underway on the Ferris place. The March winds play wild music on the telephone wires. Rain and warm winds seek out all the banks of snow hidden beneath the trees and turn it into more water for the creek. The young calves kick their heels and run in circles around the pasture. The buds on the trees puff up until a faint green fuzz of baby leaf shows beneath the brown husks. The crocus and grape hyacinth poke pale green shoots up through the dirt, unfold their leaves and lay bare the white sac at the center of their stalks so the sunlight can turn it into a flower. Day by day, as each tiny step toward springtime is made, there are more and more jobs for each member of the family to do.

David often helps with the milking

John has to milk the cows every morning and afternoon, seven days a week. Each morning, the milk is carried off to the Middleburg creamery by truck. The milking job alone, what with feeding the cattle, cleaning out their stalls, and sterilizing the milk equipment, takes four hours of every day. The rest of the day he spends in oiling and repairing tractors, harrows and other machines for spring planting. Often, he goes back to the barns after supper, and works long after Betsy and David and Peggy are in bed.

Everybody else works too. Mother and Betsy are almost as busy tending the baby chicks as they were in caring for the incubator.

David, once the seeds are sorted, goes to work on the flower beds and gardens beside the house. Margaret loves roses. She has dozens of bushes growing along the south side of the house. Roses, as everybody knows, grow from one year to another, like a tree or a bush. They are "perennials." The stalks of climbing roses and ramblers, such as Silver Moon and Paul Scarlet, must be wrapped in straw each winter to protect them from the frosts.

In March, David unwraps the straw and carries it off to the big "mulch" box at the rear of the garden. He rakes the straw off the strawberry bed and the asparagus patch too. He does this very carefully so that the teeth of the rake don't tear any strawberry plants out of the ground or bruise the pink tips of asparagus stalks forming just beneath the surface of the soil. Finally, the leaves packed around the astors, delphinium, Canterbury bells, and other perennials in the flower beds have to be raked away. So do the leaves that flew down the hill from the wood lot and up against the foundations of the house during the winter storms.

All the leaves go into the mulch box to become fertilizer. When David has finished, he goes down to the seed room in the barn and opens one of the bags of powdered limestone standing in the corner. He fills a pail half full of limestone, then adds double handfuls of nitrogen and potash and two double handfuls of phosphate. He mixes it all carefully in the pail, carries it back to the mulch box and sprinkles it across the leaves and straw. He stirs the whole gooey mess up with a shovel, then hurries off to the chicken house.

"All finished with the yard," he shouts to Mother as he comes through the door. "Now, may I run Ol' Putt-putt?"

"I get to do half of it, if Mommy says yes," Betsy calls from the corner beside the baby chicks.

"All right," Mother nodded. "Daddy oiled it just a few days ago. Wheel it up from the garage before you start the motor though."

Ol' Putt-putt, as Betsy and David call it, is the garden tractor John bought last year. It has a one-cylinder engine that goes putt-putt like an outboard motor. Half-a-dozen attachments came with it. Each one is needed as the job of growing vegetables in the garden progresses through spring and summer.

John plowed and fertilized the whole garden last fall. Last week, when he oiled the garden tractor, he attached the row of curved steel teeth called a "harrow."

At the edge of the garden, Betsy stepped on Ol' Putt-putt's starter pedal. The little engine coughed, sighed, then suddenly began to putt-putt and move forward.

The steel harrow teeth kicked into the brown waves of soil the big plow had left last fall. They broke up the clumps of dirt and scattered them evenly. Up and down, laughing and squabbling about their "turns," they tromped behind Ol' Putt-putt until dinnertime. By then the garden's surface was almost as smooth as a billiard table.

Next afternoon, [ ] and Betsy carried armfuls of short stakes and a long piece of string out to the garden. Mother had drawn a diagram of the garden on paper, showing where each kind of vegetable was to be planted. And Betsy, with her toy set of rubber type, printed the name of each vegetable on the wooden sticks. Betsy and David set the stakes exactly where the seeds were to be sown and they stretched the string across the garden, between each pair of stakes, to make certain the rows would be straight.

This job finished, they carried dozens of long poles, made from young maple trees, and sank them deep in the soft loam, in rows across the far end of the garden. The Kentucky wonders, the limas and other pole beans will climb these poles, while flowering and growing their crops.

The ground is warm enough for planting, John decided at supper. "You three plant the garden after school tomorrow," he said over the apple pie. "Then you can help me plant corn on Saturday. After all, time's getting on. First thing we know, it will be the middle of April." His lips twitched a bit at the corners. "April . . . May . . . June," he said, slowly. "David, haven't you got a birthday around that time?"

"June sixteenth," shouted David. "And you knew it all the time too!"

"June sixteenth, really," Betsy assumed a lofty tone. "I say, young fellow, do you know how old you'll be?"

"Old enough to throw you ␣␣␣␣␣ my shoulder, I bet," David said.

Betsy nodded and started talking to Peggy. Something, David knew, was going on. The secret must be about his birthday. In that case, he thought, it would be more fun not to pay any attention to Betsy's teasing. Sooner or later, she'd get excited and start dropping hints.

After supper, when Peggy had been tucked away for the night, John brought two big sacks of seed potatoes into the kitchen. He spread newspapers on the floor and put tin buckets on them. Everybody took a paring knife out of the sink drawer, and began to cut the potatoes into "seed." You have often seen potatoes sprouting. Sometimes they push out white shoots while they are lying in bins in the grocery store. Each shoot starts from an "eye" in the potato. Each eye is a seed. But farmers "play safe" and cut up seed potatoes so that there are at least two eyes in each piece. About two quarts of potato pieces are used to plant a fifty-foot row.

When Mother came back downstairs from Peggy's room, she got the electric popcorn machine down from the pantry shelf. John waved a potato in the air and said "Hurrah!" Betsy rushed out to the refrigerator and brought in the butter dish. Soon the kitchen was filled with the ambrosial odor of hot buttered popcorn. There were big bowls of it alongside each of their chairs. The only sounds in the room were "crunch, crunch,

70

crunch," and the steady "thlub, thlub, thlub" of seed potato pieces dropping in the buckets. It was a wonderful party. Nobody thought of it as "work."

Next morning, while Betsy and David were in school, John soaked the potato cuttings in a disinfectant solution, then sprinkled them with sulphur. This would keep bugs away during the first weeks of growth. He planted the potatoes himself. This work was too heavy for the children or Margaret.

The radish, beet, carrot, lettuce, onion, Swiss chard, endive, and spinach seed went into the garden that afternoon, each kind in its own marked rows. A quarter-to a half-inch of dirt was swept over each row and tamped down. Margaret had planted the tomato, cabbage, sweet pepper, and Chinese cabbage seed in the glass-enclosed cold frame beside the henhouse a few mornings before. These would be transplanted into the garden when they reached a growth of six or seven inches. The beans would be planted in early May, after the ground was thoroughly warm and there wasn't any danger of light frosts at night.

Down in the corn and rye and broccoli fields, John used his big harrow just as Betsy, David, and Peggy used the little one on Ol' Putt-putt to prepare the garden. On Saturday morning, they all helped to load bags of corn seed on the truck. The big fields spread brownly warm before them. The grass was an inch high in the pasture. Up along the hill line, the apple orchard and wood lot trees had dressed themselves in fuzzy green leaves.

Holding Peggy between them, Betsy and David sat atop the bags of corn on the bumpy, swaying ride through the barnyard and down the lane to the edge of the harrowed field. They pushed the bags, "clump," to the ground. John drove the truck back to the barn. Soon he reappeared riding the tractor, hauling an oblong box on wheels. The box has long steel tubes, set on springs, hanging from its bottom. It is a seed drill.

The children untied the bags of corn for John to lift up and empty into the seed drill's long box. Then—while Peggy made a face and held her nose, and Betsy said "Phew! I almost feel sorry for the bugs"—David put on leather gloves, scooped black powder from a big bag, and mixed it through the kernels of corn. The powder is an organic compound that protects seeds and young roots from bugs and parasites during the first weeks of growth. It has a strong "rotten egg" smell, too, that keeps crows and other "flying robbers" from digging the corn up and eating it.

Finally John lowered the cover on the box, climbed into the tractor and shifted into low gear. As he drove out across the field, the tubes and springs beneath the seed drill made a noise as though fifty people with sets of steel teeth were chattering from the cold. Every few inches, one of the tubes plunged down into the earth, dropped a corn seed, and bounced up again. Thus, faster than a man can walk, two rows of corn are planted at one time.

David, Betsy, and Peggy looked out across the field. They thought of the tiny spark of life that lay waiting in each seed. Soon the minerals, water, and warmth would cause the seeds to burst and push up yellow buds on a white stalk. They would push up through the bits of crumbled rock and powdered leaf, on and on up to the surface and the magic sunlight.

This is planting time—the season of the earth's re-awakening, and the first quarter of the farm's big game.

Chapter 6

GROWING TIME

June 16 was a Saturday. So David worked in the garden all the morning of his ninth birthday. He ran Ol' Putt-putt up and down the rows between the young plants. This time Putt-putt was wearing its cultivator attachment. It looked like a half dozen toy plows set in a V-formation on a steel frame. The tiny plows tore up all the weeds growing between the rows of crops. That saved the moisture and fertilizer in the soil for use by the crops.

After the rows were cultivated, dirt had to be pulled up around the potato plants with a hoe.

David thought about his birthday as he worked. Everybody had wished him "Happy Birthday" at breakfast. John had raised his glass of orange juice and said, very gravely, "May number nine be the best one yet, sir." Mother had kissed him on the cheek and said

74

there "might" be something special for dinner (a chocolate cake with whipped cream frosting, maybe . . . Wow! . . . I hope!). Peggy gave him two packages of her favorite chewing gum, wrapped in bright green paper. Betsy had held her hands behind her back and demanded a penny. She'd wrestled a bit, then he had to go upstairs and get the penny from his purse before she gave him the little box with the Boy Scout knife in it. He'd always wanted one, so if girls believed in that old superstition about pennies and "sharp-edged gifts," it was all right with him. The knife had cost her $3.50 from her egg money. He knew because he'd often stared longingly at it in the window of the big hardware store in Middleburg.

It was all swell—but not a thing from Mother or Dad. And when he'd asked to go down into the cornfield to help Dad that morning, Mother and Betsy had looked hard at one another, with Betsy shrieking "Oh, Mother!" Then they both giggled, and Mother said he'd better go out and cultivate the garden. David thought, "Women are funny sometimes!"

Fifty feet away, beside the stone wall, the strawberries were like red jewels strewn through their clusters of glossy green leaves. Up the garden, row on row, the carrots, beets, onions, spinach, and other vegetables draped the distinctive leaves that the sun, chlorophyll, minerals, and water had built from the tiny seeds planted two months before. The tiny black pellets of

75

carrot seed had produced tall graceful leaves like green lace. The broad, dark leaves and scarlet stalks of the beets, the bright green tubes of the onions that looked like pointed soda-straws—all of them followed a rigid pattern of growth laid down in the heart of the seed the year before.

Every beet looks like every other beet. No red beet ever looks like an orange carrot, or a cream-colored horse-radish or a green cucumber. Nor does a cucumber ever look like a beet.

This family resemblance is called a "strain."

The way each plant is to look is determined the summer before, inside the seed produced by the mother plant. Every seed contains, beneath its shell, a supply of oil and starch to keep it alive during the time it is out of the ground. Alongside this "pantry" is the tiny bundle of minerals that will produce the stalk, flowers and fruit from one end and the root system from the other end. The "family resemblance" of the plant is determined while the seed is being formed, by spindle-shaped growths called "genes." Each gene is one three-millionth of an inch long. Strings of genes wrap themselves around each other in more kinds of knots than a Boy Scout leader can tie. The genes in a beet seed make one combination of knots. The genes in a carrot seed make another combination of knots.

The shape of the knot, scientists believe, determines the kind of plant that will grow from it.

David pulled the dirt up around the potato vines, with quick, careful movements of his hoe. The potato is a fruit, like a peach or an apple. It ripens on underground branches. Unless dirt covers the growing potatoes, sunlight will cause them to turn green like the rest of the plant. So David pulled the dirt up into "hills" to assure a crop of smooth, brown-skinned potatoes that would be pure white inside, without green spots.

The screen door at the kitchen side of the house slammed. Betsy ran down the path, her pigtails flying. The blue apron she wore over her dress billowed like the sail of a small boat. "It's coming," she shouted. "The Brysons just phoned and said it had finished at their place."

As she ran past David toward the barns, he smelled strawberry jam. Then he saw the red stains on her hands. So that's what was happening to all the berries he picked yesterday. "Oh, boy," he murmured, and ran over and stood the hoe against the stone wall. (He turned its blade toward the wall so that nobody would step on it and get whacked alongside the head by the handle.)

He was halfway toward the barn when he heard a roar in the sky, and saw a helicopter skim low across a hedgerow at the far end of the cornfield. It looked like a huge grasshopper, with a cane balanced upright on the back of its neck.

This side of the hedgerow, at the very edge of the

Farmers use helicopters to spray harmful insects

corn, the 'copter settled down, leisurely and gently, until it hovered four feet off the ground, just above the tips of the leaves. Then it moved forward, at about the speed of an automobile in second gear. Out behind it, billowed a cloud of white dust.

The 'copter was spraying a chemical over the cornfield to destroy the eggs of a worm called "the corn borer." The corn was too high for a tractor to move through it without crushing many of the stalks. So David's father and other farmers of the neighborhood had hired the wingless flying machine to spray their corn from the air. Then nothing would be injured but the worms.

Insects, David has learned from experience, are one of the great menaces of the farm during the growing season. From the moment the seeds sprout, insects of all

kinds come crawling, buzzin
sweet juices of the plants. Ev
own particular bug enemies
cabbage worms, apple worn
cotton plants—and on and or

Some insects have horny
bodies and look like miniatu
brightly colored and look li
red and green and blue pebbl
hungry, dark clouds to devou
their path. Some creep decept
ing the fall, sleep in the groun
there, ready to destroy, when

Back and forth across the
John Ferris' aerial attack ag
ley on the hillside apple orc'
ing a tractor back and for
nozzles on the big tank rolli
squirted a spray high into th
pillars and gypsy moths.

Growing season is a beautif
green and lush. The skies are
breezes whisper through the
out from the buds with a hund
tingling odors. The creeks and la
reflecting every cloud and bird a
them.

But through it all, the bugs continu

ner fights back with machines
all his quarterback skill.
helicopter, Betsy suddenly re-
y jam bubbling on the back of
e on in," she called to David.
of something yummy. We've
ch of jam with maple sugar,

r," David shouted, and started
pen" the sound of his footbeats
nded up the path.

ry jam.
hey're fine with lamb).

og —
ows.

owns in tassels,
right."

d so luscious, four bumblebees were
ens on the kitchen door screen. David
eet ahead of Betsy.
ng so fast that he skidded halfway across

the fresh wax on the kitchen linoleum. Mother stood beside the sink, ladling the ruby red jam into glass jars. A tall man stood beside the stove licking the jam spoon. He turned around and looked down at David. "Why, hello there, Little David," he said.

It was "Big David" Putnam, the county agent.

"Young man," said Big David, giving the spoon another lick, "I have it on direct authority that you are nine years old today."

"Yes, sir," Little David said and gulped.

"Mmm," Big David said as he took a whopping big spoonful of jam out of the kettle, "you know anything about cattle?"

"I know about dairy cattle. How could I help but know? But I don't know anything about beef cattle because there aren't any around here."

"Oh, I dunno about that," Big David said with a grin. "Come on down to the barn and let's talk some more about this."

Big David led the way down the walk and across the road to the barn. There was a big red truck parked there. When they got to the barn door, Big David put his hand on Little David's shoulder. "Dave boy," he said gently, "when you were born I wrote you a little note. Did your Dad ever show it to you?"

"Oh, yes," David's eyes were suddenly big. "Gee whillakers—you said when I was nine years old—"

"That's right," Big David nodded. "When you were

born, I thought I'd just wait awhile and then get something for you that you could really grow up with. So-oo-o, come on in and see what you can see."

Inside the barn two men stood down at the far end of the stanchions, beside the calf pen. They looked at David and smiled. Something moved in the calf pen too. David could see it clearer now. He broke into a run.

It was a cow—a big cow with short legs and a square body and heavy fur that, in the sunlight coming through the windows, looked as red as a bed of coals. And alongside it, its red legs spread out like a rocking horse's and its white face as impudent and bug-eyed as a puppy's, stood a calf.

David leaned down and stared through the bars. He reached an arm through. The calf looked him up and down, moved forward, then gently sniffed the palm of his hand. David stared, gulped, and stared again. Pictures of both mother and calf swam up into his memory out of the pages of the farm magazines. He turned and blinked at Big David. And there were Daddy and Mother and Betsy and Peggy all standing there too.

"Oh, gee, gosh, Mr. David," he whispered. "Those are Herefords. Are—are they really mine?"

"Mr. Ferris, sir," said Big David, "there are now two beef cattle in Kerhonkson County. They are registered, sir, with the American Hereford Association in Kansas City, Missouri. And they are registered in your name. Happy birthday, Li'l David."

"Oh, golly! Oh, gee whiz! I dunno—" David rubbed a fist across his eyes. They were wet. His voice trembled. "Thank you so very much. But—what about—I mean—criminity, it's going to take a lot of feed and they'll have to be housed and cared for—and I'll work like the very dickens but . . ."

"That's all settled, David," Daddy's voice was very gentle. "This is going to be an experiment to see whether beef cattle will do well here in the valley. They've been raising them over in Pennsylvania. Big David and I think they can be raised here. I'll furnish the feed, bedding, and housing for them. That's your birthday present from Mother and me. But you'll have to be absolutely responsible for taking care of them. If you keep them healthy and fatten them out, their sales price will be all yours. Then if you want to keep on in the beef cattle business, we'll talk about it."

"Next year," Big David said, "you'll be old enough to join the 4-H club. There's one Ferris there now." He nodded toward Betsy, "She's showing some mighty nice pullets and jams at the fairs. I'd like to see you at next year's show, too, with two good-looking beeves."

David clambered over the rail. He walked slowly

toward the cow and calf. They stared at him, backed away a step, then stood still. He moved his hands up slowly and began to rub the foreheads of each one. "I— I'll do anything to keep 'm," he said, without turning.

"Lunchtime," Mother said gaily. "You can come right back here afterward, David. Mr. Putnam and these other gentlemen will want to tell you about feeds and pasture and those things."

The little group turned and walked back beside the stanchions. David was last. He kept staring back over his shoulder at the Herefords.

Dave Putnam threw a hand over John Ferris' shoulder. "Guess we got a new man on the team," he said.

John just smiled.

Chapter 7
HARVESTTIME

FROM JULY through October, the farm's crops ripen
fast. This is the third quarter of the game. Everybody on the team wants to roll up a big score. The oat
heads are golden and ripe before all the hay has been
mowed. The peas practically burst their pods, just as
the clover comes into red and white flower. The broccoli and the wheat race each other toward the goal line.
The pullets and pigs seem to double in size every two or
three weeks. The peaches and apples try to outblush
one another. The cucumbers, peppers, beets, potatoes,
sweet corn, tomatoes, and carrots are suddenly full
grown—each demanding to be picked at once and either
sent to market or processed into a hundred kinds of
toothsome foods.

This year, as usual, Grandma and Grandpa Ferris
drove out from Middleburg to take over the big cool

bedroom on the north side of the house and help out on some of the plays. As soon as he got to the farm, Grandpa heaved a long, satisfied sigh and stared out the window toward the wheat field. The harvester flashed its big paddle wheel in the sunlight as it snipped off the golden grain and whisked it backward up the chute to the machinery that separates seeds from stems. Grandpa Ferris heaved another long sigh, reached into his pocket for his pipe and hurried off downstairs, then out toward the barns.

Meantime a truck was backing down the lane. Betsy stood in the poultry house door. She waved to Grandpa and called, "Granddad, will you ask Daddy if he can possibly come up for a few minutes? The buyers are here. I want him to look over my culls and see if I've done it right."

Grandpa nodded and headed across the barnyard toward the wheat field. David trudged out along the edge of the field ahead of him, carrying a bucket of cracked corn. The two Herefords stood beside the fence two fields over, as though they were waiting for him. Grandpa stuck the empty pipe back in his mouth and grinned. Dinah and Murphy and David. They'd almost become triplets in the past two months. David was handling them just as though he'd been born on the range, instead of in old dairy country 2,000 miles back East.

It was David himself who, the afternoon of his birthday, had suggested "Dinah" as the name for the mother cow. Because, he'd said, they had a record of the song with Al Jolson singing it and, like the Dinah in the song, there wasn't anything finer than a thoroughbred Hereford.

Then Big Dave and Grandpa had gotten their heads together and suggested to David that it just might be a good idea to give the calf a real appropriate name, since it was kind of a pioneer. How about, they said, naming the calf for the great Revolutionary scout, Timothy Murphy? He'd been a leader in the Indian fighting, not more than five miles away, when the Iroquois warriors came down and tried to burn the settlers' wheat fields in 1776 and again in '77 and '78.

So, "Dinah" and "Murphy" it was. And David had really pitched in. Poison weeds, bloat, screwworms, blackleg, Bang's disease, pneumonia—all of these and other natural enemies lay, like a horde of painted Iroquois warriors, along the path of any beef calf struggling up toward adulthood. It was a big enough job for a man, let alone a nine-year-old boy.

But there they stood, up there at the fence, growing fatter and sassier every day on the diet David fed them, the currycombings he gave them and the safeguarding medicines he teased down Murphy's wriggling throat.

Grandpa Ferris shook his head, grinned and hurried off across the field. John was driving the harvester. A truck, grinding along in first gear, paced the big machine slowly down the field. The wheat seeds tumbled from the cleaning screens through a chute into the body of the truck. When the truck was filled with wheat, John stopped the harvester for a moment. The truck shifted into second gear, then into high and hurried off toward the storage bins beside the railroad tracks in Middleburg. A second truck rolled out from the end of the field, to take its place beside the harvester.

Grandpa Ferris waved at John. "I'll take over there for a turn," he called. "Betsy wants you up at the henhouse right away. Jim Green's showed up to take her pullets. I guess she wants you to sit in on the deal."

"Be good to stretch my legs a bit," John said and climbed down off the seat. "Just about an hour's work left here, anyway. You want to finish off? I'll get on with the milking. I'd like to go up and have a look at that broccoli patch before dinner. If this weather holds for a day or two, it'll be ready for cutting."

"Boy's work," Grandpa Ferris sniffed. "Why, I used to do this with a four-horse team." He leaned down, turned the switch and kicked the starter pedal. "Giddap, there, Cyrus McCormick," he yelled. The harvester rolled off, the truck bustled into position alongside.

Betsy and Jim Green, the poultry buyer, were out in the fenced chicken run. Betsy had selected fifty hens and pullets from her flock. She was going to sell them. Good poultry producers do this two or three times a year. It is called "culling." The spring chicks have

88

grown into long-legged young hens and roosters, that weigh one and a half to two pounds apiece. The young pullets will begin to lay eggs before long.

Betsy needs only five or six roosters to keep up her supply of baby chicks. And some of the hens don't lay as many eggs as some of the others. The fifty chickens she is going to market are the young roosters, and the hens that have the poorest egg production records.

The hens to be kept are out "on range," roving across the barnyard and through the fields. They are eating clover, grass clippings, weed seeds, wriggly grasshoppers, and bugs. A few of these, and a rooster or two, stare curiously back through the fence toward their doomed relatives.

John looked the flock over carefully, then gave his approval. "We get twenty back, don't we?" he asked.

"Mother says twenty-five," Betsy said. "I've got it written down here: ten stew-hens and fifteen broilers."

"Okay," John nodded. "You're the boss. I'll get along with the milking."

Jim nodded. He and his helper went off to get the empty crates out of the truck. They would slaughter and dress the fifty chickens at their plant in Middleburg. The twenty-five to come back to the Ferris place would be dressed, wrapped and quick-frozen. Then Margaret could pop them right into the quick-freeze room, for use when needed. Jim could sell the feathers and the viscera of the chickens to manufacturers. So he didn't charge anything for this job. The other twenty-five chickens would be sold to poultry dealers. Betsy would be paid for them.

By suppertime the wheat field was an expanse of golden stubble where the chickens argued with the catbirds and sparrows over the grain spilled from the harvester. Jim Green had disappeared toward town, with much cackling and small talk from the fifty stew-hens and broilers, and a farewell salute from two of the roosters. Murphy stands sprawl-legged in the pasture, staring unblinkingly up the hill at the apple orchard, his nose tilted toward the fragrance of the ripening fruit.

The next day, the produce merchant from Oneonta and his picking crew showed up early in the morning. John and Grandpa walked up and down the broccoli field with him. They examined the bright green stalks and big umbrellalike buds of the plants. The merchant offered a price for the entire crop. John and Grandpa named a figure $300 higher. The merchant grinned and raised his price another $100. Grandpa and John shook their heads and lowered their price $100. "Okay," the buyer said, grinning, "we'll split the difference. I've got to get this crew to work." It happened that way every year—everybody seemed happier doing it that way. It is called "bargaining."

The pickers carried knives with short curved blades.

They cut off the big umbrellalike buds seven inches down the stalk and tossed them down between the rows. Other workers picked them up, tied three or four stalks into a bundle and packed them in crates. The produce merchant had bought the broccoli crop "in the field." He paid the cutting crew. That saved John all the time and bother of rounding up a crew, supervising their work and trucking the crop into town.

Margaret, of course, had five crates of the broccoli delivered to the kitchen. She, Grandma, and Betsy worked all afternoon. They washed it, cut it up and "blanched" it in big kettles over boiling water. Then they cooled it fast in a bucket of ice water and packed it in quart containers. Peggy and Betsy carried the containers into the quick-freeze room and stood them on the shelves beside the cartons of peas, strawberries, cherries, rhubarb, and string beans that had been harvested during the past few weeks.

John and Grandpa hadn't been back to the barns for a half hour when the corn-chopper crew drove into the yard, and began to set up their equipment. They backed the chopping machine up to the silo, and attached the belt that drives it to the "power take-off" on the tractor. Then they ran a pipe from the chopper up to the little door at the top of the silo.

That afternoon, Grandpa drove the mowing machine around the alfalfa field. John and David took a truck up into the apple orchard and gave the fruit its sixth and last spraying of the summer. They used a mixture containing arsenate of lead, hydrated lime, and nicotine sulphate. These minerals protect the ripening fruit from two particularly mean enemies—the codling moth and the leaf hopper.

Next morning, after the sun had dried the alfalfa for a couple of hours, Grandpa drove the hay rig down into the field. Betsy and David were raking the sweet, bright green alfalfa into piles. Over in the cornfield, John and two men from the chopping crew swished their machetes down the rows.

Betsy, David, and Grandpa loaded the hay rig with alfalfa and drove it back to the silage chopper. Grandpa unhitched the tractor, hitched it on to an empty rig and drove off to the cornfield. When he returned with a load of the tall cornstalks and their half-ripe ears, the chopper crew started their tractor. They fed both the alfalfa and the green corn into the chopper. The whirling knives inside the machine sliced it into pieces no larger than a nickel; a blast of air blew it up the long tube into the silo. When the wagons were empty, Grandpa drove back for more loads. One of the men from the chopper crew opened a trap door near the bottom of the silo and climbed inside. He jumped up and down on the fragrant particles of chopped corn and alfalfa and stomped them down hard against the silo walls.

When the silo was one-third filled, the chopper crew

put on rubber boots, opened gallon tins of molasses and climbed up into the silo with it. They poured the molasses slowly down through the silage. Molasses is as good for cows as it is for humans. It contains lots of iron and other minerals we need. Also, the sugar in the molasses acts on the grass and corn juices to make them ferment and ripen.

Grass silage is a fairly new kind of feed on the farm. John is one of the first farmers in Kerhonkson County to make it. It prevents the sun from robbing the farmer of much of his crop's goodness.

For thousands of years, farmers cut their hay, raked it into little mounds (called "cocks") and then—praying that it wouldn't rain—let it dry out until it was ready to store in the haymow.

But we now know the green in all growing things is "chlorophyll." And chlorophyll is rich in vitamins. When the grass is cut, the tiny "mouths" on the leaves fall open. The sun pulls out the wet chlorophyll, just the way it pulls (or evaporates) other moisture on a hot day. That is why hay turns from bright green to pale yellow when left in the field.

But grass chopped and put up into a silo with corn is still moist. It holds on to a good share of its chlorophyll and vitamins. Cows and horses need to eat some dry hay, too, to help them digest their food. But grass silage is almost as rich as grain. It saves the farmer money when he has a lot of animals to feed all winter long.

More and more farmers are putting part of their grass and clover into silage every year.

Many farmers, too, are building a new kind of silo, called a "trench silo." They dig a big hole in a hillside, and line it with concrete. Then they blow the silage into this hole, and cover it over with tar paper and a little dirt. All winter long, then, they can actually "mine" silage out of the hillside.

So, through the hot, bright days of August and early September the crops raced toward the goal line . . . some of them delayed by the traffic jam they created for John, Grandpa, David, and Betsy—others postponed a day or two by growling thunderstorms and rain. Tomatoes, carrots, beets, potatoes, apples, plums—all came pouring in as though the sun, readying for its journey back toward the equator, suddenly pulled a string and dropped all the goodness and fine smells and bold, booming colors of the rainbow right down into the farmhouse and barns.

After the apples had been picked and washed in big tubs of muriatic solution to remove the spray powders from their skins, they were trucked off to the cold storage warehouse in town. Then the pace began to slacken a bit.

The silo was filled. The haymow was stacked with fresh bales of wheat, straw, and hay. The quick-freeze room fairly bulged with cartons of goodness. The potatoes were dug, and stored in a dark bin in the cellar.

About the only thing left was the corn picking. For now the fields stood almost bare again, ready for their winter's rest. Once again the grains and vegetables and trees had struggled mightily against bugs and drought and sudden storms to produce the seeds that mean continuance of their life in the next growing season. And in so doing, they had produced food and fiber for man.

This was the great urge of the farm year—the gigantic rush for the goal line of harvest, the urge for the big score. Now, with harvest, the year's job was done.

Chapter 8

THE SEASON OF REPAIR

On a sunny Friday afternoon in October, Betsy and David raced up the walk from the school bus and dashed upstairs to change their clothes.

"Hurry," Betsy called to David from her room. "Mother says we're going to have an early dinner. The corn pickers are coming out tomorrow morning, first thing."

In almost no time they were both ready for the afternoon project—nut gathering.

"Oh, boy," David said as he ran around the barn and down the lane toward the orchard, "d'you suppose we'll have a machine picker over?"

"Mommy says so," Betsy panted. "There'll be a lot of people over to see it."

"Won't take us an hour to do this," David said, swinging open the orchard gate. "I've got to feed

Murphy and Dinah, anyway. Gleeps, if we're going to have a lot of people around, I guess I'd better rub'm down, too."

They trudged off up the hill toward the hickory tree that stood at the very crest of the hill. It was a very old tree. That is why it stood alone. Its dense branches and leaves absorbed all the sunlight. Other trees near by could not get enough light to grow big.

The leaves of the oak trees had turned a red brighter than a fireman's shirt. The maple and elm leaves were varying shades of yellow and dusky gold. The weeds beneath them had wilted to a cinnamon brown, just like the bean and tomato plants in the garden behind the house.

And now, with every breeze that rustled across the brow of the hill, hundreds of tree leaves came tumbling down, until the ground was knee deep in a crisp, rustling carpet of scarlet and gold, yellow and mauve.

The perennials have grown a little bit larger during the growing season. The tree trunks are a half-inch thicker than they were in March. Each year's growth is marked off inside the trunk and branches by a thin brown line. A broad, light-colored layer of wood is grown during the growing season. The thin brown line is created by the slow circulation of water and chemicals inside the bark each winter. When farmers cut down a tree, they can tell just how old it is by counting these "annual rings."

When the frosts come and the sun is far away in the sky, most trees, bushes, and other perennials proceed to take down their drapes, and put up their shutters. Only the thick-skinned needles of the pines and evergreens can survive the winter frosts. The other trees pump a layer of wax across the stem of every leaf. This, like a shutter, seals off the interior of the plant.

Some people say that the leaves of these trees and plants die at the end of summer. They don't though. When the tree has pulled its waxy shutters tight and snuggled down for the winter, the leaves relax and put on holiday clothes. The cold nights cause chemical changes so that every leaf switches from green to a gay color. The leaves of oak trees and sumac turn a bright red. The leaves of maples and most shrubs turn yellow. So do the grasses.

Day by day, these leaf colors grow brighter across all the hillsides and orchards and yards of the farms. Then, when the winds blow, the crisp wax wall at the leaf's attachment to the stem is broken. The leaf swirls gracefully down, twisting and skimming and looping with the ease of a bright-colored bird.

On the ground, these leaves join the stems and leaves of the annual plants. They crumble and gradually become part of the soil. Thus they really do not die. Next year, or the year after, some of their chemicals will be carried back up the tree from the roots to build into leaves again.

That is one of the big reasons why the period of the year between October and March is the season of repair on the farm. The dropping of the leaves gave the name "fall" to the months of September, October, and November. The winds and rains and snows that follow during December, January, and February gave the name "winter" to that time of year, because "winter" is an old German word that means "the wet season."

So from leaf fall until planting time, the leaves turn slowly back to chemicals and soil, the ground collects rain water, and the trees and bushes relax from their big game.

"Hurry, David," Betsy called from above. "The squirrels will have all the nuts."

"Yeah. Gee!" David turned to watch Daddy on the tractor, hauling a disk back and forth across the wheat field. The sharp round blades cut the roots and bases of the stalks into small pieces, then pulled them into the ground. This was part of repair season too. The chopped bits would rot during the fall rains and winter snows. By spring they would be a pulpy mass that the plows and harrows could break into still finer fragments. Thus the wheat stalks turned into soil and released their fibers and chemicals back to the earth, so that other seeds might grow there.

Something rustled in a tree above David's head. He looked up to meet the unblinking gaze of a pair of beady eyes. A squirrel, standing head down on the tree trunk, stared at him. The squirrel's cheeks puffed out as though it had a bad case of mumps.

"So-o-o," David shouted, just as if the squirrel could understand him. "You are getting at those hickory nuts, aren't you? Well, you don't get all of them, mister." He broke into a dead run, up the hill after Betsy.

Within a half hour Betsy and David each had a sack half full of nuts. Betsy took a piece of string from her pocket and tied it around the mouth of her sack. Then she turned the sack on its side and picked it up by the middle. Half of the nuts fell toward the top and half toward the bottom. She balanced the empty middle of the sack over her right shoulder, and started down the hill with both hands free.

But David carried his sack boy-style. He twisted the top of the bag, grabbed it with both hands and heaved it up on his back. Then he trudged off down the hill after Betsy.

Walking an imaginary line up through the barnyard, they stopped to peer in the garage door. The harvester, the other tractor, the seed drill, plow, and harrow were back in a corner, bundled away for the winter beneath canvas covers. Stacked on the floor, beside the welding machine, were a set of broken springs, a new plow point, the cutter bar from the mowing machine, and some other tool parts that needed repair.

Here, in the months of snow and wind ahead, John and perhaps Grandpa would do the "fixing up" on machines for the next spring and summer's work. Too, there was the incubator to put back into running order, the other tractor to be overhauled, an extension to be built on the chicken house. And, come icicles big as your arm, or snowdrifts to your neck, the cows had to be fed and milked every day; the chickens and pigs, Dinah and Murphy must be "tended." There are no eight-hour days on a diversified farm, no winter layoffs or summer vacations. It is a good life, but it means hard work most days of the year—and work of all kinds.

David sniffed as they came up the walk toward the kitchen. Daddy was right. There was going to be pumpkin pie for dinner. He put the bag of nuts down in the woodshed, and ran back to the barn. John had just finished milking the last cow, and was carrying the milking machines out to the "springhouse" to wash. David picked up his feed pails from the calf pen. He poured approximately six pounds of cracked corn into one pail, then went off to the corner of the barn beside the silo, pulled up the trap door and shoveled the other pail full of silage.

He carried the pails out across the barnyard and dumped them through the fence into the feedbox Grandpa had built for Dinah and Murphy. Then he went back to the calf pen, took the currycomb off its hook, stuck it in his hip-pocket and picked up an armful of clover hay from the pile at the foot of the "mow chute."

He tossed the hay through the fence, climbed over and pulled the currycomb out of his pocket. Then he gently ran the comb over the Herefords' shoulders and bellies while they ate. The comb pulled out very little loose hair this time of year, because the animals were growing their heavy winter coats.

But Murphy had taken a nap in a burdock patch sometime during the day. His coat was matted with burs. The currycomb got them all out. It quickened the blood circulation in his skin, too. His fur fairly gleamed in the late afternoon sunlight. As if by way of "thank you," Murphy turned his head and began to nibble at a pocket of David's trousers. Then he held very still while David rubbed his head from nose to ears and back again.

Dinah looked up just once from the feedbox, and switched her tail as though to say, "Humbug. Child's play."

David was washing his hands and face for supper when a car stopped; familiar footsteps sounded on the walk. Grandma Ferris came into the kitchen all smiles. Behind her, Grandpa carried a big paper bag in his arms. "Betsy," he said, "suppose you pick up that bag and get right to work. Few dirty socks and a couple of nightshirts in there. I thought you could wash 'em up before supper." He disappeared into the hallway.

Betsy picked up the bag and peered inside. "Mmm,"

she exclaimed. "What delicious socks!" Grandma had made them a batch of ginger cookies!

The next morning, while they were all still at breakfast, automobiles began to pull into the barnyard. A few minutes later a machine that looked like a lobster came up the road. It had big steel claws sticking out from each side of its body. They were orange-colored.

"There's the corn picker," David shouted. "Let's go."

"Ooh," Betsy said as she peered out of the window at the big lumbering machine. "What a goofy-looking thing. Is Daddy going to buy it?"

"I doubt it, dear," her mother answered. "They cost a lot of money. Maybe twelve or more farmers could buy it together, and your father might go in on that."

David and Betsy, with Peggy between them, went down to the edge of the cornfield. Grandpa, Daddy, and the other men were wandering around the machine, peering underneath it and trying its levers and gears. Pretty soon the salesman climbed into the seat and pushed a button. The big claw-like arms raised up until they were level with the top of the cornstalks. Everybody stood back then, except Bill Blair and Frank Weems, two young farmers from down the valley. They said they'd like to race the machine, just for the fun of it. The salesman grinned and nodded.

The two young farmers tied leather mittens, faced with steel wire, on their left hands so that the sharp

The corn picker's steel claws snipped off the yellow ears

kernels and stalks of the dried corn would not cut their skin.

Corn, when it reaches full growth and produces yellow kernels on the ear, begins to wilt. Its job is finished. All its life has passed on to the yellow kernels. These will grow other stalks of corn next year. So with life gone, the stalks and leaves fade in the fall winds and slanting sunlight. The sun and wind pull the moisture out of them. The kernels in the ear dry up, too, except for the flicker of life in the knotty genes, resting beside their oily food supply beneath the plastic skin.

The machine roared and lurched forward. The steel claws rustled through the dry stalks, shook the husks loose, snipped off the big yellow ears and rolled them up a webbed belt into a wagon traveling alongside.

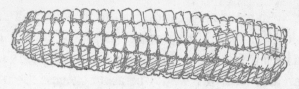

Two rows away the young farmers raced down the field. They tore the ears loose from the stalks with their gloved hands and tossed them "bang" against a board that stood four feet above the box of the wagon traveling beside them. The sun-dried ears made a noise like a gunshot when they hit the board. Many of the kernels broke away from the cobs and sprinkled across the wagon floor. That is why "bang board" has only one meaning to farmers. It is the board that stands high above the wagons at corn picking time.

The machine finished picking two rows before the young farmers were halfway down the field. After that the machine rumbled on alone.

At lunchtime, everybody had sandwiches and milk at a long table set up in the front yard. Margaret and Grandma served tarts too. They were hot from the oven, and spread with the strawberry jam made with maple sugar. The corn picker salesman said his wife was one of the judges for the jam and pickle displays at the County Fair. He wanted Margaret to make some more jam next summer, and enter it in the contest. He said Margaret's was the best he'd ever tasted.

On the way back to the cornfield, Grandpa took some of the men over to visit Dinah and Murphy. Bill

Blair, who went to a training camp in Montana during World War II, said they were "as pretty" as any Herefords he saw out there. The salesman said he sure hoped Dinah and Murphy would be a big success, because if more Kerhonkson farmers raised beef cattle, they'd grow more corn for feed. "Then," he grinned, "mebbe I can sell you fellows some of these danged steel lobsters."

By nightfall, the machine had picked all the corn. The round, galvanized steel "crib" beside the henhouse was filled to the roof with the yellow gold kernels and cobs.

After supper, Grandpa and John went to the little steel safe in the corner of the kitchen, and took out the farm's record books. Margaret and Grandma cleared the kitchen table. John sharpened a pencil and tilted back in his chair. "Well, kids," he said, and smiled. "This is it. One more load of pigs to market, and harvest's about over. You run along to bed while we see what the year's score is."

David stayed awake a long time, listening to the low hum of voices from the kitchen. Farmers work hard the year around, he thought. They play the game with all the spunk they have in them and use all the new plays they can discover to beat the bugs, the storms, and the drought. But they really don't know what the score is until the game is all over—because farmers sell their products for money. And after the crops leave the farm a lot of things can happen to make prices low. Sometimes, when the costs of bags and boxes and fertilizers and machinery and cow feed are high but sales prices are low, farmers lose money. That, Grandpa said, was really why the co-operatives were organized a long time ago.

The next morning, when Betsy and David woke up, the ground was white with snow. Winter was on the way. Now farmer and land alike were in the season of repair.

Chapter 9
THE CROPS GO TO MARKET

OUTDOORS, a truck ground up the curving drive-
way into the school yard. Indoors, Dennis Siburski, who had red hair and freckles, raised his eyebrows a full inch and stared across the aisle at David.
His mouth didn't seem to move, but the whisper was
clear. "There he is!"

At the same instant, a chorus of plaintive "oinks"
sounded through the window. Somebody in the back
of the room tittered and said, very softly, "Sooey,"
which is what farmers say to pigs. Miss Miller, the
teacher, wandered over to the window, looked out and
waved. Just then, the three o'clock bell rang. Everybody
began to line up for the march down the hall to the
school busses.

"Whose pigs?" a boy asked.

"Ours," said David. "We're going down to the
auction."

"My father's already down there," Dennis Siburski announced in a loud voice. "I'm riding down with David to meet him."

The announcement brought only a small rumble of approval from the assemblage. Dennis elevated his eyebrows again and, with great poise, crossed his eyes until everybody stared at him. "The Ferrises got Chester White hogs," he announced. "We got Durocs. My father says Durocs are a better bacon hog than Chester Whites."

An admiring young lady named Sylvancia Fitzburger, who had blonde curls and china blue eyes and two warts, nodded agreement and asked Dennis to cross his eyes again. Miss Miller came down the line. "All right, David," she smiled, "you and Dennis may go now. Your father's waiting for you. Tell him I think those are splendid-looking Chesters."

"Yes'm," said David. "Miss Miller, aren't Chesters just as good as Durocs?" Miss Miller was also a "leader" in the 4-H club. She would know.

"They're both very good breeds," Miss Miller said. "From a marketing standpoint there isn't much difference between them. They're good neighbors, anyway. The Chesters originated in Pennsylvania and the Durocs came from New Jersey."

"Thank you," David looked at Dennis and gave a decisive nod. "Will you be sure to remind Betsy that if she wants to meet us after 4-H meeting Daddy and I will be over at Mr. Putnam's office just about five?"

"I imagine she'll ride home with your mother," Miss Miller said. "There's a home demonstration meeting here at the school this afternoon. She'll probably go with her."

The pigs poked pink snouts inquisitively through the slats of the truck body. They blinked, and said, "Oink," when David and Dennis raced down the steps.

"Here we go," John said as they climbed into the cab beside him. "Mother's at a meeting. Betsy's at a meeting. I've got four errands to do, and we've got to be home for milking by 5:30 at the latest. That's what I like about living in the country. You never have anything to do—just sit around all day and twiddle."

"We've got a twiddle," Dennis began with his blank, innocent stare. "Daddy says when I grow up, I can take twiddle lessons. If . . ."

"Daddy," David stuck his fingers in his ears. "He goes on like that all the time. Put him out back with the pigs."

"I'm too young to shave," Dennis said, and crossed his eyes. "You can have your razorback."

John groaned and honked a greeting to Harry Malone as they swung past the traffic light.

The Middleburg Livestock Auction Sales Association, Inc. is a half mile out of town on the Bangdale road. It is a long, low building where farmers bring their cows, pigs, and sheep to sell to traders and meat

Farmers often sell their livestock at auctions

packers. The organization is a co-operative, and is owned jointly by 300 farmers in Kerhonkson County.

The meat we buy at the butcher shop has been sold and resold several times before it reaches the shop. When Grandpa Ferris was a young man, Kerhonkson farmers sold their livestock to "country buyers" who drove them off on foot to the railroad siding at Middleburg. The animals were loaded in big, slatted "double-decked" freight cars. They were shipped off to stockyards in Jersey City, or Buffalo. Sometimes they went as far as Cleveland or Chicago. There the animals were herded in big wooden pens in the open air and put under the supervision of an agent of the "country buyer." This agent charged a five or ten per cent commission on all the animals he sold. So he was known as a "commission man."

Millions of animals are still sold by this method. The largest stockyards in the United States are at Chicago, Kansas City, Denver, Fort Worth, South St. Paul, and Omaha. The commission men still operate there. Some of them, such as the firm of John Clay, have a splendid reputation among farmers. Every morning and afternoon, agents of the big meat-packing firms, such as Swift, Armour, and Cudahy, ride on horseback along the lanes between the pens. These agents are very knowing. They buy thousands of heads of livestock every day and can usually tell at a glance just how well the animals have been treated and what qualities of meat will be found on their carcasses. They are the official "buyers" for the meat packers. They name the price they can afford to pay for each pen full of animals.

After the sale is made, the animals are driven off over elevated runways built of iron and wood to the meat packers' factories near by to be turned into meat, leather, glue, bone meal, fertilizer, chemicals, and hundreds of other products.

Not so long ago some farmers decided they might be able to get more of the packers' price for their animals if they banded together and formed their own sales organizations. When John Ferris and other farmers around Middleburg decided to start an auction barn, each farmer put up $50. That was only $15,000 from 300 farmers. The land and buildings would cost $30,-000, and they would probably need another $25,000 for operating expenses before the business showed a profit. They arranged for a $40,000 loan from the Farm Credit Administration, a branch of the U. S. Department of Agriculture created to encourage farmer-owned businesses.

These farmer-owned livestock co-operatives now sell about sixteen million animals each year and do over a billion dollars' worth of business.

The inside of an auction barn looks like a miniature race track at a fairground. There is a big open space with sawdust on the floor, and a fence around it. Behind the fence are rows of bleacher seats.

The auctioneer, a fat man with a tan fedora hat on the back of his head and a big blue handkerchief clutched in his left hand, stood on a little platform at one end of the sawdust ring.

A herd of thirty spotted black and white Poland China pigs ambled back and forth across the ring. The auctioneer mopped his face with the blue kerchief and began to chant, "Twenty, twenty, twenty. Fine a lot of pigs as been in this ring today. There's no rind on that bacon, gentlemen. You just speak gentle to 'm an' they'll roll right over an' start to douse themselves with brown sugar. Twenty-three-dollar hogs if I ever saw any. Twenty, twenty—hah, gent'mun says twenty-one. Twenty-one, twenty-one. Thank you, sir, twenty-one-fifty. Twenty-one-fifty."

The buyers from the packing houses sat on the

bleachers, along with the farmers. Whenever a buyer decided he wanted the herd of pigs in the ring, he signaled with a wave of his hand, or sometimes by just winking. That raised the bid another dollar or half-dollar, according to the kind of signal he made. The auctioneer had to watch every movement of these buyers—and keep them interested at the same time. That's why auctioneers usually carry big handkerchiefs and keep pitchers of water near them. They work hard.

The herd of Poland Chinas finally sold at "twenty-two." In other words, the buyer was paying $22 per 100 pounds for the thirty pigs in the ring. Each pig weighed 225 pounds. So the farmer who sold them would receive a check for $1,485, minus the sales commission charged by the co-operative.

The Middleburg "barn" had already earned enough through these commissions to pay back $35,000 of the $40,000 borrowed from the Farm Credit Administration. After the debt is paid off, the auction barn profits will be turned over to the 300 farmer-owners each year in the form of "dividends," just as other companies pay dividends to their stockholders.

A man bustled in through a side door and handed John a small slip of paper. It read, "John Ferris . . . 8160." That was the weigh slip on the thirty-four Chesters. They had weighed a total of 8,160 pounds. John slipped it into his pocket, and waved "hello" to some of his friends. He and David hurried back to the truck. When the pigs were sold, that day or the next, the buyer would pay the manager of the auction barn, and the Association would send John his check. John was smiling. With pigs selling at $22 or better, the truckload of Chesters would make a good profit, even though feed prices were high.

They drove back to Middleburg and down to the G.L.F.-Center beside the railroad tracks. G.L.F. is the nickname for Grange-League-Federation. It is the big farmer-owned co-operative in New York State, just as "Eastern States Farmers Exchange" is the principal farmer co-op in New England, and "Ohio Farm Bureau" is the principal one in Ohio. G.L.F. was founded by The Grange, The Farm Bureau Federation and the Dairymen's League. So the names of all three were put together, and the initial nickname followed.

All told there are more than twelve thousand farmer-owned co-operatives in the U. S. A. today. All of them are based on the law, "One member—one vote." This is called the Rochedale Principle, after the factory workers in Rochedale, England, who thought up the idea of co-operatives a century ago. Sweden, Norway, and Denmark are the only countries in the world that have as large, and as important, farmer co-operatives as the U. S. A.

Some of our farm co-operatives deal only in the fur and yarn spun from the Angora rabbits the members

raise. Other co-operatives are formed by cranberry growers. There are corn grower co-operatives, cattle co-operatives, wheat co-operatives and even co-operatives that sell lighting, fire, and automobile insurance.

The G.L.F.-Center at Middleburg includes a locker plant where farmers can have livestock butchered and the meat smoked or quick-frozen for their home use. Each member has a locker, like the gym lockers in school, where, if he doesn't have a quick-freeze room at home, he can store all his frozen foods.

This idea was thought up by a great farm leader at Ithaca, N. Y., named H. E. Babcock. "Ed" Babcock was the general manager of the G.L.F. co-operatives for many years. He nicknamed the first locker plant at Ithaca, "Mother Zero."

Next to the locker plant is the G.L.F. store that sells feeds, fertilizers, fencing materials, some building equipment, and farm machinery. Across the street, beside the railroad tracks, is the grain elevator where corn and wheat are stored. When market prices are high, in January or February, the grain will be sold, then poured into freight cars and rolled off to feed and flour mills at Buffalo or, perhaps, Minneapolis or Chicago.

Up the railroad tracks from the grain elevators is the

big, sprawling building of the Kerhonkson Valley Cold Storage Association. And beyond that are the tall smokestacks and big windows of the creamery.

As John and David, with two pigs in the truck, drove up to the locker plant, a steam engine backed into the creamery siding and clanged into the five black railroad cars standing there. These were refrigerator cars, loaded with the day's supply of milk. Some of it came from the Ferris' herd. By midnight the milk would be in the huge pasteurizing and bottling plant on Fifty-seventh Street in New York City. And by four o'clock next morning, most of it would stand in quart containers on doorsteps all over the city.

John backed the truck up to the locker plant platform. The two pigs stared curiously as a man in a white coat came out on the platform, and grinned. "There they are," John called. "Margaret says no smoked shoulders. Put it all into the sausage. And a little more smoke on the hams. Dad chanted like a Comanche last time, because they weren't dry enough."

John climbed down from the truck to help unload the pigs. The butchers at the locker plant would slaughter them and cut the carcasses up into bacon, hams, spareribs, "fat back," loins, and sausage meat. The head would be boiled with herbs. Then its tender meat and juices would be poured off and processed into headcheese. The sausage meat would be ground up with sage and other spices, and wrapped in two-pound packages and frozen. The loins, livers, hearts, and knuckles, wrapped separately and quick-frozen, would be ready whenever Margaret decided to use them. The fat back, soaked in a salt solution, would become "salt pork." The hams and bacon, inoculated and rubbed down with hickory salt and sugar, would hang for days over a slow fire of corn cobs and hickory wood chips until they were the color of waxed mahogany on the outside, and a pungent pink inside.

David stared across the tracks toward the cold storage plant. Over there, all their apples from the September harvest were actually snoozing. Scientists have discovered that apples, pears, and similar fruit will "go to sleep" if they are given plenty of carbon dioxide (that is, "stale breath") and kept in a temperature of 33 degrees—just one degree above freezing. So the fruit growers of the Kerhonkson Valley organized a cold storage association and put up a building—very much as the auction barn was financed and built.

The inside of the cold storage plant is a series of refrigerator rooms. At harvesttime, apples are stored in these rooms. Each room is sealed off. Carbon dioxide is pumped in. The refrigerator dials are set for a steady temperature of 33 degrees. The apples "go to sleep." Molds and bacteria that form in fruit at higher temperatures can't operate at 33 degrees. So the fruit doesn't rot or wilt. It stays "fresh."

Two, or six, or seven months later, whenever the city

fruit dealers need them, the apples are taken out of storage, loaded into refrigerated railroad cars or trucks and rushed off to the city. Thus, everybody can have a fresh apple any day of the year.

With shrill protest, the Ferris' two pigs disappeared inside the locker plant. John backed the truck around to the loading platform of the G.L.F. store. It was soon loaded with "wet mash," a feed of mixed cornmeal, oatmeal, and buckwheat for Betsy's chickens, and big bags of protein meal and cottonseed meal for Dinah. Also John bought some shingles for the roof of the chicken house addition.

They drove out along Railroad Avenue to the County Courthouse. Big Dave Putnam's office was on the second floor, at the end of a pea green corridor. The sign on the door said "U. S. Department of Agriculture. Extension Service. David Putnam, County Agent. Rebecca Delaney, Home Demonstration Agent."

Just as they arrived, Big Dave charged through the office door, a sheaf of papers under one arm. "Greetings, greetings," he roared as he sat down. "Two things —and then I've got to drive to Oneonta for a dinner meeting."

"Just take your time," John looked at his wrist watch. "We haven't got a thing to do except get home, unload a truck of feed and begin milking twenty-two minutes from now."

Big Dave shook his head. "I always knew you'd slow

down one of these days. That shouldn't take you over eighteen minutes. Lookie, how's chances on holding a discussion meeting out at your place in January? I'd like to get a bunch of fellows together to go over this whole beef cow proposition. We can show 'em Dinah and Murphy—let 'em look at the records—and see what they think of the whole idea. After all, we're close to the Albany and New York City markets here. Good chance for some of these fellows to pick up a little extra money. It might encourage them to grow better grass, too."

"Margaret will have my scalp," John sighed. "She's entertaining the home demonstration group on January twelfth, and Betsy's 4-H club will be there on the eighteenth. I sorta planned to go up to the Friends of the Land convention the week of the tenth, if we can persuade Grandpa to take over the milking."

"Mmm," said Big David, frowning. "I'd hoped we could have the meeting on the eighteenth."

"Okay," John said. "If we're going to do it, we might as well do it good. Besides, David's been saying he wanted to talk 4-H with you and maybe that will be a good chance."

Both Daves looked very pleased.

As John and little David came out of the courthouse door, the milk train blew for the crossing. And down Main Street, a big silvery truck, loaded with cases of eggs and apples roared off down the highway toward New York City.

Chapter 10

FUN ON THE FARM

B Y THREE o'clock on the afternoon of Betsy's 4-H meeting, the Ferris house was spick and span. A chocolate cake, gleaming in its heavy frosting of whipped cream like the snow-covered hillside, stood on the sideboard in the dining room. Grandma had colored some of the frosting green and squirted the big four-leaf clover emblem of 4-H on its top.

Buttermilk biscuits, shaped and in their pans, waited in the refrigerator for the arrival of Big Dave and the farm neighbors that evening. Four frozen chickens, carrots, peas, potatoes, butter, and white sauce had disappeared into the innards of the three great dishes of pot-pie waiting on the back of the stove. The containers of raspberries for the shortcake thawed on the pantry shelf. But until suppertime, Betsy's gang would take over.

4-H members learn about farming by "doing"

Nearly two million farm boys and girls belong to 4-H clubs. City children can form their own clubs and join too, if they wish. Members must be between ten and twenty-one years of age. Each member takes the 4-H oath to "pledge my *head* to clearer thinking, my *heart* to greater loyalty, my *hands* to larger service, my *health* to better living for my club, my community, and my country."

There are 4-H clubs in some European countries too, and in Asia, Africa, and South America. In Great Britain, Canada, and Africa, they are called Young Farmers clubs. In Cuba, they are known as the 5-C clubs, and in Venezuela as the 5-V clubs. But wherever they are, all the members work and study together, to show what they can do for themselves and for their neighbors, through programs of self-help. They learn about farming, homemaking and community activities by "doing."

In the U. S. A. each year, more than five hundred thousand 4-H members study methods to prevent forest fires, barn fires, injuries from sharp farm tools, and auto accidents. Another group, almost as large, studies methods for conserving fish, birds, wild animals, and harmless snakes in the country. They also learn plowing and cropping methods that will reduce soil erosion.

Members of 4-H clubs grow more than a million acres of field and garden crops each year, care for more than 1,000,000 head of livestock, preserve more than 16,000,000 quarts of food, and "put down" 3,000,000 pounds of quick-frozen products. Each member has his or her own "special project," just as Betsy's chickens are her project, and Murphy will be David's project.

Through funds supplied by wealthy people and manufacturers who are interested in 4-H work, members judged to have unusually good projects each fall are sent to the National 4-H Club Congress in Chicago. During this week, usually in November, at the same time the International Livestock Exposition is held at the Chicago stockyards, the champion cattle, pigs, sheep, chickens, canned goods, dresses, maps, and other projects of the 4-H members are judged by expert men and women in each field, and National Championships are determined.

The girls meeting with Miss Miller at the Ferrises

are studying soil conservation. They went into the living room for their discussion, after crows of delight over the chocolate cake and its green decoration.

David hurried down to the barn to look after Murphy and Dinah. At least twenty people would be at the night meeting. He wanted the animals to look as well-groomed and slicked up as anybody. Murphy had grown like a weed. Daddy said he would weigh over six hundred pounds on the scales at the auction barn. His red and white hair gleamed. He held his head proudly. There was a mischievous look in his big, unblinking eyes.

Within a few months, Murphy would be known as a "yearling steer." He wasn't a bull, because of an operation he had back on the range, before Big Dave bought him. Steers can't have children. But they grow bigger and produce tenderer meat than bulls. And steers are safe for young boys to manage, even when they reach their full growth of twelve or fifteen hundred pounds.

If Murphy was a bull, neither John nor Big Dave would have permitted David to have him. Bulls, all farm people know, are almost as dangerous as a lion or a tiger. Farm bulls, necessary for the production of calves, are kept in strong "paddocks" or fenced yards. Even Peggy knows better than to go near the paddock where John keeps their big, 2,000-pound Holstein bull. Whenever John goes into the bull's paddock, he carries a stick with a steel snap on the end of it. He hooks the snap over the ring on the bull's nose. Then, if the bull starts to charge, John twists the stick. That hurts the bull's nose, and he calms down.

David finished currycombing Murphy and Dinah. They looked as good as the pictures of the prize animals in *The Farmers Handbook*. He grinned, hung the currycomb back on its hook and ran off to the house. Mother said he could have a piece of the girls' cake.

The meeting was over. Miss Miller was cutting the cake. Everybody had glasses of cold milk. Betsy and two other girls were mixing sugar, water and cinnamon to make the syrup for the candied apples. While they ate cake, and said "mmmmm" and rolled their eyes, the cinnamon syrup bubbled on the stove. Finally, Betsy dropped a spoonful in a glass of cold water. It turned solid, and dropped "clink" against the bottom of the glass.

Big, red Northern Spy and Golden Delicious apples had been washed and stood on the sink. The girls picked each apple up by the stem, dropped it in the hot syrup and swirled it around. Then they fished it out with a spoon and stood it on a paper towel, for the cinnamon taffy coating to cool.

Miss Miller decided there was time to play a game called "word garden." It was a new game she had read about in the Dairymen's League magazine. The girls divided into two teams.

"If you plant an angry wise man, what will you raise?" Miss Miller asked Helen Dalrymple.

Helen didn't know. A girl on the second team raised her hand. "Scarlet sage?" she asked.

"That's right." Miss Miller nodded. "That's the way it goes. Now, Betsy, what will you raise if you plant days, months, and hours?"

"Days, months, and hours?" Betsy frowned.

David, eating his cake in the doorway, giggled. "What time is it, Betsy?" he asked.

"Oh—oh—thyme, the herb."

"That's right," Miss Miller shook a finger at David. "No more kibitzing from the balcony, young man."

"I'll be quiet," he grinned. "I've got to go back to the barn and help Daddy."

He was just putting his hat and overshoes on when Peggy trotted in from outdoors. "Me give Murphy present," she announced.

"That's nice," David said absently. "What did you give him?"

"Evreebuddy eat taffy apples. Me give Murphy taffy apple, too. He liked it. Only make him cough a little."

"He what?" David asked, very slowly.

"Murphy cough," and Peggy coughed a little to show David what she meant.

David's heart sank clear to the bottom of his stomach. He stamped into his overshoes and raced toward the barn. Murphy stood in the far corner of the pen. His legs were spread apart; his head was down. He opened his mouth, coughed, gasped and coughed again. Dinah stood across the pen staring at him.

David climbed over the rail. He wanted to lie down in the straw and cry. He put an arm around Murphy's neck and pulled the calf's head back. Then, he reached his left hand gently into her mouth and wriggled two fingers down her throat. The sticky taffy crust of the apple was lodged halfway down. It was too far down to pull it back, or even push it on through toward her stomach.

"Choke," he said aloud. That's what farmers call it when an apple or a potato or a solid mass of food lodges in a cow's throat. It can choke the animal to death in an hour, or sooner.

What was it? Somewhere—somehow he had heard or read what to do in case of "choke." It was—it was—*The Farmers Handbook*. Something about rubber hose, rubber hose and vaseline. Was that it?

David turned, climbed back across the fence and raced toward the springhouse. There was a piece of hose there. Daddy used it to flush the concrete floor. And he kept a jar of cold cream on the shelf, for chapped hands in the wintertime. The hose wasn't very clean. It would have to do.

He unscrewed the hose from the faucet, took down the jar of cold cream, and scooped up a fistful. His hands trembled so much he could hardly hold it. He smeared the cold cream all over two feet of the hose, and ran back to Murphy. Murphy still stood with his head down. His eyes were rolling. He gasped and wheezed and coughed.

David pulled the head upright, propped the mouth open, then pushed the greased hose gently and very slowly down Murphy's throat. It stopped and bent as it hit the apple. He pushed harder. The hose bent again. Murphy swung his head. His eyes were popping. He looked exactly like a baby screwing its face up to cry.

David wriggled the hose and pushed. The apple turned half over. Another inch of hose. Another push. The apple began to move steadily downwards. Suddenly, Murphy gagged, and gave a great rib-shaking cough. Out popped the hose. David went suddenly weak. He let the hose lie there in the straw. He put both arms around Murphy's neck, and started to cry.

"Well done, Li'l David," Big Dave said softly across the fence. "He'll be as fit as a fiddle now."

David looked up, and rubbed his eyes. Big Dave and Daddy stood beside the pen looking at him. They didn't look a bit unhappy. They looked as proud as a pair of Betsy's roosters.

"By golly," Big Dave said, "Ol' Professor Osborne would have passed that one. As neat a job of choke-cure as I've seen in years."

"B-plus, at least," Daddy nodded, then hopped across

the fence and put an arm around David. "Murphy's going to be all right, son. I'm awfully darned proud of the way you handled it. Look at the old rascal."

David peered out through his father's arms. Murphy had his head up. The mischievous look was back in his eyes. He drew a deep breath, pointed his pink nose in the air and bellowed "mawww," at the top of his lungs. Dinah switched her tail once, rolled her eyes and bent down again to her clover hay.

Soon after supper that night the first cars bringing farmers to the cattle meeting drove into the yard. The women and children stomped in through the kitchen door. Each family carried a bowl of potato salad, or a jar of pickled pears, or a three-tiered layer cake, a container of ice cream, or loaves of homemade oatmeal and amadama bread as gingerly as though each were a week-old baby. These were each family's contribution to the "snack" to be served at eleven o'clock. It was, in a way, something like a co-operative. Each farm supplied one share. Alone, it didn't seem like much. Yet when all the families had arrived, Margaret's kitchen looked like opening day in the Homemaker's Building at the Kerhonkson County Fair.

Most families brought their children and babies with them. The babies were wrapped in blankets and laid in two rows on the big maple four-poster bed in the front guest room. Marjorie Evans, who was going to go to nursing school right after she graduated from high school in June, presided from the rocker at the far end of the room—a magazine and a big pile of clean diapers alongside her.

The toddler gang disappeared in Peggy's room, more or less under the supervision of Miss Mulhauser.

The larger children used Betsy's room as a cloakroom and general headquarters but spent the first half hour examining the new bicycles Betsy and David had gotten for Christmas. Then they decided to go down to the barn where the men were and have a look at Murphy and Dinah. Betsy went to look for David to come with them.

"He went out the side door about ten minutes ago," one of the boys told her. "After all, it's his calf. I'd want to be down there, too."

David knew that, as a host, he should be polite to the other children and show them around. He did his best, too—except that he kept staring out the window into the yard where the men had gathered in little groups, smoking and talking. Then when he looked again, they were drifting off toward the barn, with Big Dave and Daddy in the lead.

Of course, Murphy was all right! Daddy had said he was all right. But if he wasn't all right—and the men got there—and Murphy was down on the straw, slobbering and coughing again—and his eyes rolling. That was silly, but . . .

Almost before David knew it, he had his hat on and was flying down the path toward the stanchion room door. The lights were on. The Holsteins and Jerseys stared sleepily, some still standing, others lying down. The men clustered around the pen at the far end.

Suddenly he saw a small, square white and red head between them. The pink nose pointed straight up toward the rafters. Murphy said, "Mawwww."

"By durn," Frank Dalrymple was saying, "they're purty things, aren't they? You know, I read somewhere that they feed 'm on alfalfa and grass in the Argentine. Fattens up just as good as corn, they say."

"Well," Big Dave rolled his eyes. "You might get into an argument with some people on that. But one thing's certain. We could use a lot more pasture land in this county if we had some beef cattle. And it would do a lot of this low-production cropland good to rest up on grass for a few years."

"Heh," Jerry Fesca shook his head. "They say farmers were the founders of civilization. Well, here's our chance to do some refounding."

"By Harry," old Mr. Kirkpatrick spoke up, "if a nine-year-old boy can do a job like this, I think it's high time some of us old bucks shook a leg, too."

Nobody had seen David. He didn't want anybody to see him. It was worth a million dollars just to hear Murphy bawl that way again, and to have people say those things about him. He tiptoed back out of the barn.

Chapter 11

CROPS AROUND THE COUNTRY

OFF TO THE LEFT, beyond the big black shadow of the Union Station in Washington, D. C., rises the gleaming dome of the Capitol. Beyond it rears the giant white spire of the Washington Monument, built nearly a hundred years ago as a memorial by the American people to the Virginia farm boy who became "The Father of our Country."

Halfway between the Capitol and the Monument, behind the strange castlelike towers of the Smithsonian Institution, stand the two white marble and granite buildings that are the home of the U. S. Department of Agriculture. More than eighty thousand people are employed by this department. The county agents, the 4-H clubs, the big experimental farms at Beltsville, Maryland and Albany, California; the agricultural laboratories in Louisiana, California, Illinois, and

132

Pennsylvania are all directed from here. All eighty thousand of these men and women employed by our government are working hard to make the farm a better place to live and to improve our soils, water supplies, crops, and livestock so that the American people will never have to worry about starvation.

It's interesting to note that the street that runs from the Agriculture buildings over toward the Capitol is called Independence Avenue—for a lot of our independence really did come out of the farm.

Historically, American agriculture is like a tree with many branches but with only three roots. The branches are, of course, the different kinds of farms we have today: wheat and cattle and fruit "ranches"; cotton, tobacco, sweet potato, sugar cane, and rice "plantations"; apple, peach, cherry, plum, or pear "orchards"; grape "vineyards"; vegetable "truck farms"; sheep "ranges"; hog farms and, of course, diversified farms such as the Ferrises live on.

The three roots, or beginnings, of all these farms form a triangle. One grew from the North, another from the South, and the third from the West. Each root came from times long ago.

The past that gave rise to the three great roots of American farming are still very much alive in us. The English farmers who settled on the warm, rich coastland of Virginia after 1609 discovered that their soils would grow excellent crops of tobacco, rice, and cotton.

Since each of these crops requires a different type of soil and growing condition, these farmers tended to specialize in raising one kind of crop. Also, most of these farmers had a personal dislike for the word "farm" because hundreds of years ago the word meant a plot of land that is rented. So the Virginians and Carolinians and Georgians called themselves "planters." Quite naturally, then, their land holdings were known as plantations.

A generation after the Virginians started their plantations, a band of Puritans sailed from Plymouth, England. They, too, hoped to settle in the pleasant lands of Virginia. But the captain of the ship, the *Mayflower*, landed them on the coast of Massachusetts Bay, 600 miles north.

The Massachusetts winters were, and are, long and very cold. The Massachusetts fields were filled with stones. The hills were covered with forests of pine, hemlock, oak, maple, and chestnut. The Pilgrim Fathers could not grow cotton, peanuts, rice, or tobacco on their land. They never had the big, level fields on which to grow large crops. Instead, they learned to make their living through diversification.

Thus, long before George Washington's day, two systems of agriculture originated in America. Diversification came out of the rocky fields of New England. One-crop agriculture came out of the lush, broad fields of Virginia and the southland.

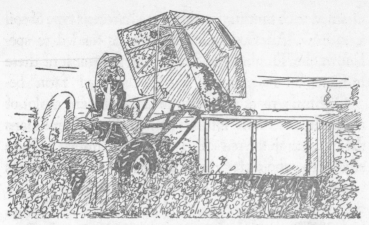

Modern cotton growers often use picking machines

These became two of the principal roots of our farming tradition. The third root, originating from the West, was the farming discoveries of the American Indian. For it was the Indians from across the Pacific who settled America from west to east, before the white man and the black man came across the Atlantic and settled America from east to west.

Let us take an imaginary trip across country on a streamliner and see what farms across the country look like. Our capital in Washington is a good place to start from.

As our silver streamliner roars southward over plantations and beside mountains where these farming traditions began, its headlights flash across fields where men and women, working wearily to pluck the "bolls" of white fiber from the cotton plants, first made up and chanted such spiritual melodies as "Swing Low, Sweet Chariot," "All God's Chillun Got Shoes," "Nobody Knows the Trouble I've Seen," and "One More River to Cross."

Our train roars through the star-spattered darkness past hillsides where tobacco plants poke velvety green shoots through the red soil. The South Carolina swamps are green where, for three hundred years, black and white men alike have fought alligators and poisonous snakes to grow crops of rice and vegetables in the boggy, black fields along the coast.

Traveling west, the Great Smoky Mountains pile green-blue shadows against the sky. This is the country of the popular songs "Turkey in the Straw" and "Shortenin' Bread"—of hillside fields "so steep the mules have got longer legs on the downside than they have on the upside," or so the mountain people say.

Across Georgia, the countryside changes to mile on mile of peach orchards and flat, red fields where the weak little shoots of peanut plants lie like young clover. Some of the farm homes have no paint and broken-down autos stand in their muddy yards. Others are bright new bungalows with flowers in the yards and tractors standing by the barnyard gate. When the houses are run down, the fields look sick and worn out. But when the houses are bright and cheerful, the crops and fields look perkier and healthier.

As we speed south in our streamliner, the grass grows

taller and the tree leaves bigger. The orchards give way to the pinewoods and vegetable farms of North Florida. Soon we are rolling past groves of orange trees and lanes of coconut palm that look like giant gray-green feather dusters stuck upright in the earth.

Orange farmers have as difficult a year-round job as the diversified farmers back in Middleburg. Orange trees begin to bear fruit the third year after they are planted. The fruit takes two years to grow. The blossoms, green fruit, and ripe fruit are all on the tree at the same time.

The fruit must be protected "all the way" from bugs, "blights" and the possibilities of cold weather sweeping down from the north. Big kerosene lamps called "smudge pots" are a necessary tool in orange farming. When the Weather Bureau announces a cold wave is on the way, the smudge pots are set on the ground among the trees and lighted. The thick, oily smoke they give off hangs in a black, warm cloud above the orchard and keeps the air above 32 degrees.

Let's leave the train a little and take a bus trip through the beautiful jungles of the Everglades swamp to plantations where sugar cane is grown. Sugar cane looks like bulrushes, or cornstalks, but grows ten to twelve feet high. Sugar and molasses are made by boiling down, and straining, the juices pressed from the ripe stalks. Until a few years ago, sugar cane was harvested by hand. Workmen cut it with long, broad-handled knives called "machetes." Now much of the Florida sugar cane is harvested by machines that look like corn pickers, but are three or four times as big.

Back on the train, and heading for New Orleans, we pass fields full of a strange kind of hump-backed cattle. These are Brahmans. Ordinary cattle don't have any glands to sweat with, so they can't stand the really hot weather in this section of the country. But a few years ago, the cattlemen discovered that these hump-backed cattle from India have got sweat glands and so can stand hot weather. They brought some of them over here and crossbred them with our Shorthorns and Herefords and Angus and other beef cattle. That made it possible to turn North Florida and most of Alabama and Mississippi into beef cattle country. It's becoming as important a farm industry in the South as citrus and vegetables. They've discovered, too, that the pulp and rind left over after they've squeezed the juice out of oranges and grapefruit at the canning factories make a good livestock food. This is how, as time goes on, farming develops new ways—years ago no one would have dreamed of citrus fruit and beef cattle working in a team!

As we travel west, new pictures unfold. The dirt beyond the windows changes from black to bright red. The orange groves give way to groves of tung trees, fields of young cotton plants and hillsides of big, shadowy pecan trees that, from a distance, look very much like the hickory tree on the hilltop at the Ferris farm.

In New Orleans is the French market, beside the steamboat docks on the Mississippi. Its stalls are bright with huge strawberries from farms of the "bayou" country, stalks of yellow bananas from Central American plantations across the Gulf of Mexico, mustard greens and little bunches of sassafras root from the hill farms of Mississippi.

Beyond New Orleans, the West really takes over. East Texas is bright green with spring wheat. Tractors pull cultivators and plows across the fields. Within two months, hundreds of wheat-harvesting machines will begin their 2,000-mile march north up the heart of the continent. They, like the bugs, are really controlled by the sun. The wheat harvest ripens in South Texas in May. Then the full, golden heads roll slowly north with the sun, ending with harvests in Montana and Canada in late August and September. The "harvester brigades" follow right along.

West of San Antonio, the land is parched and dry. The mountains rise in steep, jagged cliffs of colored stone. This is the country of "Ghost Riders in the Sky," Billy the Kid, Pancho Villa, and the overland mail stagecoaches. Herds of cattle and sheep wander along the horizon. Beside the tracks, patches of cactus and desert flowers bloom in brief, bright colors before the

Huge machines harvest the Imperial Valley's crops

sun steals all the moisture the winter snows have stored
in the ground.

In California we see "the lowest farms in America."
Through sand dunes 200 feet high, we go down and
down and down until at El Centro station the land is
200 feet lower than the Pacific Ocean is at San Diego,
100 miles west beyond the mountains.

El Centro and the surrounding farmland of the Imperial Valley is the best place in America to understand
the influences of water on farming. It was desert fifty
years ago. Then settlers persuaded the Federal Government to dig a canal through the sand dunes from the
Colorado River. Today the Colorado River water irri-
gates all the fields of the Imperial Valley. The valley is
so hot in summer that most of the women and children
move out to the mountains for four months of the year,

and thermometers stand at 100 degrees at midnight. But the water has turned the lowlands into a farming paradise. The farms grow six and seven crops of alfalfa a year, and thousands of tons of fresh vegetables during fall and winter.

Water is the all-important farm tool. Even a one-day drought could cause millions of dollars' worth of crop damage. Big machines for digging irrigation ditches are as familiar a sight in the Imperial as runabout trucks are on other farms.

On and on for many hours we travel past the mountains between the valley and the sea, until we come to the rolling Pacific slope. Far in the distance, Los Angeles sprawls like a great painted forest beside the blue sea. Orange groves and vineyards cover entire mountainsides. This, too, was desert country a hundred years ago. Then some farmers came along who wanted to grow oranges and fruits. But they needed water. So they began to irrigate from the creeks and rivers, and dig wells and build reservoirs. Now California farm crops earn ten times as much every year as all the money that came out of the Gold Rush of 1849.

Here we see the largest lettuce farms in the world, where machines with arms fifty feet wide cut the heads from the field—twenty rows at a time!

As our streamliner carries us north, we speed across the sugar beet fields, the walnut orchards and vineyards of the Sacramento Valley, and on into the forests of

Flower farms grow hundreds of acres of blossoms

giant redwood trees and the rich dairy farms of Tillamook, Oregon.

From San Francisco to Portland, Portland to Seattle, Seattle across the mountains to Cheyenne—it is farms, farms, farms all the way. There are great valley farms where scores of workers stoop in the black muck to slash the green stalks of asparagus. There are upland farms where sheep and cattle roam and graze in steep pastures, and alfalfa sprouts emerald green—with the towering snow-capped mountains for a dazzling backdrop. There are farms that grow hundreds of acres of daffodils and tulips as a cash crop. There are mountain ranches where the herds of Herefords munch contentedly on the bales of hay that had been thrown to them from airplanes during the raging blizzard two weeks before. Farms, farms, farms—all sizes and shapes, all kinds, all working the year around at the huge job of food-and-materials-production, all following the rules of the game, all coached by the sun.

All kinds of farms work the year round at the job of food production

Chapter 12

COACHED BY THE SUN

As IMPORTANT as people and machines are on the farm, no crops could grow without the rest of the team—above all, the soil and the sun.

The soil in your front yard, and everywhere else, was made by the sun. The process took millions of years. And it is still going on.

There are hundreds of kinds of soil on the earth. Some kinds are red, some yellow, some blue, black, or dazzling white. All of it was made by the various kinds of influence the sun has on ocean tides and on weather. Soil is a combination of bits of stone, dried roots and leaves, and rotten wood that have been ground to powder by the action of wind, rain, frost, sunshine, and ocean tides.

The next time you are near a trolley car line, or a subway, or a railroad, look at the steel clamps that hold two

144

sections of rail together. The rail ends are not tightly joined. The track gang deliberately left a space between them. This is because the steel in the rails contracts during the cold winter months and expands under the sun's heat in summer.

Rocks act the same way. They expand during the warm days of summer, and contract during the frosty weather of winter. But in rocks there is no room for expansion and contraction. They crack and break, then crack and break again, until they are finally gritty bits of dirt. Many of the stones cracked by the frost and sun are rolled downhill into creeks and rivers by heavy rains. The water tumbles them over and over during the floods each spring and fall. It bangs them against other rocks. All this creates more dirt. Much of this is carried into the oceans. The rest is deposited along the river banks, and on the flatlands that the rivers race across during their floods.

A similar process goes on all the time in farm fields and in forests. Gardeners bundle rose bushes in straw in late fall, and pack dry leaves and moss around the roots of other shrubs. When they remove this covering the following spring, the straw, leaves and moss are wet and mushy. As it dries out, some of it will crumble to powder. This is dirt too. It was created by the sun's influence on our weather.

Dead grass and cornstalks in the farm fields, as well as leaves and dead limbs fallen from trees in the forests, all slowly turn into dirt. They follow this same slow chemical process of getting wet and drying out again, of freezing and thawing. A dead tree will turn into dirt in the same way, although it may take fifty to a hundred years. In addition to the weather, beetles, worms, slimy molds, bacteria, mushrooms, and other forms of life that live in dead wood all help the job along.

Ocean tides are created by the pull of the sun and the moon against the earth. This endless movement slowly grinds pebbles and shells along the shorelines into the bleached, white dirt we call "sea sand."

Different kinds of rocks, trees, and other matter ground into dirt by wind and weather produce different types of soil. On farms in New York, New England, and Ohio the soil is of a type called "brown forest podsolic" because great forests covered all the country from the Atlantic to Central Indiana when the Pilgrims landed at Plymouth, Massachusetts in 1621. The leaves, branches, and tree trunks that rotted there for thousands of years turned into a thick layer of crumbly, sweet-smelling brown soil.

On the prairies west of Indiana there were very few trees. For thousands of years a huge lake had covered all the land from Indiana to the Rocky Mountains. This was the ancestor of the Great Lakes. As a tough, wiry grass began to grow in this old lake bottom the water drained away down the Mississippi and St. Lawrence valleys. This grass grew four and five feet high each summer. The dead prairie grass wilted and slowly crumbled into soil each winter. In some sections, this "prairie loam" was twenty feet deep.

The South, like New England, was once covered by forests. However the soil is different, because the rocks in the South contained large quantities of iron. As the rocks crumbled, the iron stained the soil. It turned some of it a dark red, and some a circus-pink. Most of the soil south of Washington, D. C., is known as "red forest podsolic."

The sun, although it is the head coach of farming, never wrote out its plays and rules on a blackboard. Farmers had to learn them by observation.

They learned, in time, to test soil by its feel, its smell, and even by its taste. If you are ever with a farmer the first time he visits a field, you will see him reach down, pick up a handful of dirt, crush it, knead it into a ball, break the ball, then rub a few grains of it between his first finger and thumb. Each one of these gestures will tell him something about the soil in that field.

The farmers learned, too, that all of the kinds of soil could be grouped into three general categories, for crop-growing purposes. These types are "clay," "sand," and "loam."

Sandy soil is known by its coarse, gritty feel when rubbed between the fingers. Some of its rock particles are large enough to be seen with the naked eye.

Clay soil can be kneaded into a ball when it is moist. It has a greasy feeling when dry.

Loam is a mixture of sand and clay. It can be kneaded like clay, but has a gritty, sandy feel.

Wheat grows well on a heavy clay soil. Corn and barley do very well in rich loam. Rye grows best on sandy soil.

The sun, then, created the soil by its system of alternate heat and cold and wet and dry. Over thousands of years, each type of plant became accustomed to certain kinds of soil and weather or, as scientists say, "They have become adapted to it."

The roots of plants live in soil. They are as alive as the rest of the plant. Movies have been taken showing in *slow motion* the growth of roots. The movies show roots dodging around underground rocks, and wriggling like tadpoles in their search for food and water. The roots of a large tree will bore through an entire acre of ground. The hair-like roots of an alfalfa plant will push sixteen feet underground.

Roots are the foundations that hold the plant in place. They feed the tree too. All the "solid" food and water needed by the plant is taken up by the roots.

Thousands of friends and enemies of the plant live underground with the roots. The enemies are grubs, larvae, and other forms of life that eat the juices and fibers of roots. The friends include angleworms and soil bacteria. If it were possible, farmers would award medals and honorary degrees to them. Angleworms are the world's best plowmen. It has been estimated that the angleworms in one acre bring more than a ton of soil to the surface each year. The holes they dig let moisture sink deep into the land.

The tiny soil bacteria do an even more important job. They digest minerals in the soil, and turn them into chemical compounds that can be used by the plant roots. One of these families, called "nodule bacteria," manufactures nitrogen on the roots of clover and soybeans. Other bacteria turn manures into the dozens of minerals the roots search out as plant food.

The commonest soil minerals are nitrogen, phosphoric acid, potash, lime, magnesium, and sulphur. Plants also need some copper, zinc, iron, aluminum, lead, boron, beryllium, and other metals, but in such very small amounts that the scientists have named this latter group, "the trace elements." Large quantities of the first group are eaten up by plants every year. A field of corn will consume eleven pounds of potash, twenty pounds of phosphate and forty-seven pounds of nitrogen in growing fifty bushels of grain. A field of potatoes will consume seventy-seven pounds of potash, seventeen pounds of phosphate and forty-three pounds of nitrogen in growing two hundred bushels of potatoes.

The rocks and wood and leaves from which dirt is made originally contained large quantities of minerals. But, as the figures above show, each farm crop eats huge quantities of minerals. Therefore, in order to keep on growing healthy crops, farmers must spread fresh supplies of minerals over the fields each spring before plowing.

Mixtures of these minerals are called "fertilizer." The straw bedding used by cows and horses, and their manure, is often used as fertilizer on farms, because it contains large quantities of acids that the soil bacteria will manufacture into minerals. Green grasses, such as clover and alfalfa, are rich in minerals, too. Some farmers plow grasses back into the soil. They call this "green manure." The commonest kind of fertilizer, however, looks like powdered cornmeal. It can be purchased in most hardware or feed stores. These are the powdered minerals themselves, mixed like a drugstore prescription into any proportion the farmer needs. These fertilizer mixtures are sold by number. A 5-8-7 fertilizer contains five parts of nitrogen, eight parts of phosphates, and seven parts of potash. A 4-8-4 mixture (the kind most home gardeners use) is four parts of nitrogen, eight parts of phosphates, and four parts of potash.

All minerals are food and fuel for the mighty task of growing a seed into a plant.

However, essential as they are, minerals are only a fraction of the "raw material" needed by the farmer to produce his harvesttime "touchdowns."

You can prove this to your own satisfaction by a very simple experiment.

Plant seeds in a pot—not more than a half inch deep. Between the tenth and the eighteenth day, tiny sprouts will appear

Take two flowerpots, the kind with round holes in the bottom. Put a tablespoonful of dry fertilizer in each pot. Poke a half dozen garden seeds down into this fertilizer. Then stand the pots up on a dark shelf and leave them.

Nothing will happen.

Try mixing the fertilizer with dry dirt and make sure that the planted seeds are not more than a half inch below the surface of the soil. Then stand the pots back on the shelf, in the dark.

Still nothing happens.

Set the pots in a shallow pan of water. Keep enough water in this pan so that the soil is moist. Watch it for two or three weeks.

Sometime between the tenth and eighteenth day, if your seeds were alive (or, as farmers say, "fertile") tiny cream-colored and pale yellow sprouts will appear above the surface of the soil.

Now, stand one of the pots on a window sill, so that it will receive several hours of sunlight each day. Leave the other pot in the dark closet. Keep both pots watered.

The baby plants in the pot on the dark shelf may grow to be three or four inches tall. But they will be yellow and scrawny. Some of them may unfold tiny, wrinkled leaves. These will be a pale lemon color. They will look sick. Within a week or two, despite all the care you give them, these plants will collapse and die.

Meanwhile, the plants in the pot on the window sill have put out similar yellow leaves. But in a day or two, these turn a deep green-grass color. The leaves get larger. The frail, white stems become tan colored and thicker and huskier. If bugs don't attack these plants, they will grow so large that within two or three weeks, it will be necessary to dig them up, very gently separate the tangled roots and replant each one in a separate pot, or in warm ground outdoors. Within two or three months, each plant will be full-grown, or "mature." If you planted hollyhock seed, each plant will be five or six feet high at the end of three months. If you planted pansy seed, or sweet alyssum, they will be only six or eight inches high.

What have we done here? What does this farm experiment mean? Let's go back to the two pots, one on the shelf in the dark, and the other on the window sill in the sunlight.

We discovered, to begin with, that seeds will not

grow in dry fertilizer. Then we went on another step and found that they won't grow in dry fertilizer mixed with dry dirt, either. They didn't start to grow until we put water in the shallow pan and let the soil feed the seeds a constant supply of moisture.

This process in itself is one of the most important in the farmer's list of basic rules. Soil is, actually, very generous about moisture. It passes it along to its neighbors. If you wet one end of a sponge, then let it stand for a few minutes, the water will spread through the entire sponge. Soil acts the same way. The process is called "capillary attraction."

Soil feeds the roots of plants this way every time it rains or the lawn sprinkler is turned on. Brooks and rivers feed plants and trees along their shores by the same method. Irrigation ditches, which are artificial man-made brooks, do the same wetting job for farm crops in the dry plains and valleys of the Far West.

So we have proven that plants need water in order to grow. But something else, something very startling, happened after the plants began to sprout.

The plants growing in darkness on the shelf died after a few days. If we pulled one of these out of the soil and examined it, it would have looked like any other plant, in every way. It had tiny roots, no larger than a baby hair. It had a stem, or stalk. It was beginning to grow leaves.

But it died!

The plants growing in darkness will die after a few days

The only thing the pot on the shelf didn't have, and the pot on the window sill did have, was sunlight.

Sunlight is the most important thing on the farm. Seeds will sprout without it if they have enough water and fertilizer. But they will wither and die in a few days. Our football game of farming can't be played without the sun.

Until a few years ago, neither farmers nor anybody else knew *why* the sun was so important to all growth. Some people believed it was because of the warmth from summertime sunlight. Others suspected that something about the light itself caused growth. Sunlight, these few contended, contains a kind of power that can perform a very complicated manufacturing process, just as electricity lights a lamp bulb, or steam and running water drive huge wheels.

When cattle stand in open sunlight, these people

noticed, the animals will turn their heads and lick the fur on their shoulders every once in awhile. Not until scientists discovered the whole family of vitamins, did farmers learn the reason for this. Vitamin C, which the sun puts into the fruit of oranges and tomatoes in large quantities, is now nicknamed the "sunshine vitamin." The sun deposits vitamin C in the warm, moist hair along the cow's shoulders. So cows get much of their vitamin C, not by drinking orange or tomato juice, but by licking their shoulders.

Incidents such as this, observed over thousands of years and carefully put down in notebooks, gave scientists a great deal of information to begin their experiments with sunlight, twenty-five years ago. Meanwhile, microscopes, spectroscopes, and other machines were invented. These enabled the scientists to investigate tiny portions of plants and leaves. During the past few years, since the discovery of atomic energy, the Geiger counter has been used to trace the paths of fertilizer, minerals, water, and other liquids through the interior of live plants.

By all of these means, science has learned that sunshine, water, and fertilizers are three of the "raw materials" the farm needs to grow seeds into plants. Of these three, the actual coach, or power plant, if you wish to call it that, is the sun.

The sun, we know, is a huge ball of flame and molten chemicals. It is about 108 times as big as the earth, and

93,000,000 miles from the earth. It takes sunlight 498.7 seconds, or approximately eight minutes, to travel from the sun to the earth. Scientists estimate that the temperature of the sun's surface is 10,000° Fahrenheit (the kitchen oven at 350 degrees will do a fine job of cake-baking).

The light reflected to the earth across those 93,000,-000 miles is, of course, what we call "sunlight." Most of us look at sunlight as a nice kind of warmth, that brings blue skies, robins, baseball games, swimming, and picnics along with it.

But when we stop to think about it, sun heat is a form of energy. Heat will operate steam engines, cook foods, turn iron, charcoal, and lime into steel, and warm houses and office buildings during winter.

All the sunshine falling on the earth each year, the scientists have discovered, provides enough heat to give every human being 20,000 times as much heat-energy as he now uses.

Only one per cent of this energy is used to grow all the farm crops, plants, trees, and seaweed on earth. The exciting possibilities of finding use for the other 99 per cent becomes as challenging as the great, unexplored forests of Kentucky were to Daniel Boone. There is just as much pioneering to be done in sunlight exploration as was ever done in forest and prairie exploration 100 and 200 years ago.

This became more and more apparent to scientists

as they began to sleuth out, by use of their microscopes, spectroscopes, and Geiger counters, the methods used by sunlight to turn soil minerals and water into the materials that will grow plants from seeds.

They did not get very far in this search until they found that a fourth raw material comes into the picture. That raw material is air. Not any kind of air. A very particular kind. The stale air that human beings and animals breathe out. This is the fourth "basic ingredient" that sunlight uses in the process of making plants grow. Without it, we might starve to death. But we would probably choke to death first for lack of "fresh air."

Plants and animals (including mankind) actually exchange breaths with one another. That, the scientists learned, is one of the secrets of plant growth. The whole process has been given the name of "photosynthesis." The word is based on an ancient Greek word: "photos," meaning "light." Photosynthesis means "combining by the use of light."

Many of the chemical details of this immense process of photosynthesis are still unknown. As this book is written, thousands of men and women are working in laboratories trying to unravel more and more of the secrets of this and of the new "photoperiodism" (which means "response to the length of light"). Like the study of photosynthesis, this is an effort to find out just what habits the sun has created in plants—and what energies are hidden in sunlight and other forms of light. So don't be too surprised if, a few years from now, both farmers and home gardeners begin to turn white and colored lights on their growing crops for an hour or two each night in spring and summer. This will be one more pioneer venture into that wilderness of sun energy to be explored by farmers and everyone else interested in the betterment of life on earth.

Chapter 13

FARMS AROUND THE WORLD

THERE are two and one-half billion people on the earth now. Two-thirds of them (about 1,660,000,-000) live on farms of some sort, and earn their living by growing crops. If we do a little more arithmetic, we discover that there are 660 times as many farm children in other sections of the world as there are in the U.S.A. Somewhere out across the seas—in Europe, Asia, Australia, Africa, South America, and Canada—Betsy, David, and Peggy each have many "farm cousins" of their own age. But very few of these farm cousins live on the rich cropland that the Ferrises have in Middleburg.

But let's talk about the U.S.A. a bit more in order to have a better understanding of the problems farmers in some parts of the world are up against. They are our old, familiar problems of sunshine, minerals, water, machines, and topsoil.

Millions and millions of farmers on earth have only a half-team with which to play the big game.

For instance, the Ferris farm is a very old one as American farms go, but very young as compared to the farms in most of the areas of the world. A few farms along the Atlantic coast, especially in New England and Florida, are as much as three hundred years old. But more than seventy per cent of America's farms have been plowed and cropped for only 125 years, or less.

Even in these few years, as compared to the thirty thousand years of agriculture, our huge forests have been cut down and billions of tons of valuable topsoil have been washed into the rivers and oceans. (This loss of topsoil is called "erosion.") Great and sincere efforts are being made by many people who are not farmers, but who realize the land's importance, to discover methods by which the rest of our topsoil can be saved, and our worn-out, eroded fields revived. These people have formed such important organizations as the Conservation Foundation, the Friends of the Land, and many others.

Also, before looking at farms elsewhere in the world, we must remember the part that freedom plays in our daily lives. The Land-Grant Colleges were established almost a hundred years ago for the free education of farm children like John Ferris and Big Dave Putnam. The big central schools are being constructed in the farm areas all over the U.S.A. for this same reason—a better free education for farm children, so that they can be finer citizens and make better livings on their own farms when they grow up.

Huge and expensive laboratories have been organized by both the government and by industries to devise new uses for farm crops and develop better seeds and animals.

It is this "atmosphere of freedom," the historians tell us, that gave inventors such as Thomas Edison, Henry Ford, Eli Whitney, Cyrus McCormick, and others the courage to carry on their experiments, and eventually produce the tools and machines that have been of such great benefit to American farm families.

This atmosphere of freedom never developed for many of the other farmers on the earth. The land on their farms has been cropped and plowed and cropped again for thousands of years, some of it for all the thirty thousand years since farming began. The potash, phosphate, iron, copper, and other necessary minerals were used up centuries ago. All the trees were cut down, the rains washed the topsoil into the rivers, the farmland became desert and wasteland. Land-Grant Colleges have never been organized. Systems of county agents have never been set up by most governments. There are no home demonstration agents, no laboratories.

The prestige of farming, the world's very first profession and the founder of civilization, has sunk so low in most countries that seven out of every ten farmers in the world can neither read nor write; only about one-third of the farm families ever have enough to eat; half the world's farmers don't own a farm tool larger than a sickle; between a third and a half of the world's farmers die from malnutrition, exposure, or overwork before they are thirty years old.

Let us suppose that, today, we started a farm tour around the world, taking off from LaGuardia Airport in New York City (after buying a bottle of the cold, sweet milk that left the Ferris farm yesterday morning).

We will fly west in a DC-6, across the Ferris farm, on into Ohio and Illinois, across the wheat fields of Kansas, the truck and fruit farms of Colorado, the range and sugar beet country of Utah, down into the fabulously rich valleys of California and on over the blue Pacific. We are going this way, through Asia and along the Red Sea to the Bible lands, because this is where most of the world's farmers live. Here are a few of the conditions we would see along our route:

Japan. More than fifty per cent of the population are farmers. The average farm contains two and a half acres of cropland. The principal crop is rice. As one recent visitor there said, "Rice feeds the man, his family, and his animals, if he has any. It provides thatch for his hut, fuel for his fire, and rope and containers for his shipments." Japanese farmers are now averaging a production of fifty-three bushels of rice to the acre. Few Japanese farmers can earn more than $200 per year.

In many parts of Asia, rice is the principal crop

Korea. This peninsula of Asia is another region of two-acre farms. Prior to the outbreak of hostilities in 1950 between North and South Korea, the farmers of North Korea were taxed so heavily by the Communists that their taxes sometimes exceeded the total price of their harvests. The South Korean farmers work long hours for little pay, and are almost as bad off. There are few schools. Farmers here, too, rarely earn more than $5.00 a week.

China. Farming has been under way in China for at least twenty thousand years. The wheelbarrow was born in China, many centuries after the ancestors of the American Indian began their slow migration across Manchuria and the Bering Straits. The farms today are desperately poor. A typical farmer in Hunan, South China, has four children but only two acres of cropland. His total income is about $100 per year from field crops and $30 per year from poultry and pigs. Of the 27,000,000 people in Hunan, which is about the same size as Kansas, 18,000,000 live on these small farms and have average incomes of $130 per year, per family.

Siam (Thailand). We are still in the rice belt. Except for a few large plantations, most of the field labor is still done with hoes and crude knives that aren't any larger, or nearly so well made, as a pair of scissors. The soil of Siam is so overworked and undernourished that the average yield of an acre of rice is only nineteen bushels. And rice is one of the meanest crops grown. It is planted in mud, cultivated in rainstorms and usually harvested by hand, a stalk at a time. A field gang of sixty women must work a ten-hour day to harvest two and a half acres of it.

India. Many of our favorite foods originated here. Onions, cucumbers, eggplant, and sugar cane all came out of India thousands of years ago. Now much of the farmland is worn out. The tools available to farmers are pitiful. Religious beliefs prevent many of the improvements that could be made. Monkeys and cattle are both regarded as sacred by the Hindu farmers. The monkeys run wild, and destroy many of the crops. None of the cattle are used for food. Wood and coal are so expensive in India that dried cow manure is often burned in the homes for fuel. Most plows are so ancient in design that an eight-acre field is about as much land as a pair of oxen can cultivate.

Israel. Here, at the center of Bible land, we are close to the farm's birthplace. Israel today is an exciting symbol of what can be done to improve croplands, pastures, forests and the life of farm families throughout the world.

Across the deserts, a few hundred miles away, the great cities of Tyre, Nineveh and Babylon are broken pillars of stone standing in waterless wasteland. They are lessons of soil ignorance and bad farming practices. Ancient farmers there cut down the forests for wood and fuel. And they failed to put enough manures and fertilizers into their soils after harvests.

In time, the soil gave up its store of chemicals to the crops. There were no tree roots to slow down water evaporation by the hot summer sun. There were no tree leaves to manufacture new chemicals through photosynthesis. The winds rolled sand in from the southern deserts. The sand swept across fields and choked the bushes and crops. It swept into city streets and filled them, too. The great cities, that mighty armies had failed to conquer, vanished because of the trees their farmers had cut, and never replaced, centuries before.

In the few years since Israel became a republic, farming operations have leaped forward a thousand years. Ancient farming areas are being resettled by hard work and endurance as Jewish immigrants wrest little garden plots from amid the stony places. "Those who have been in Israel as long as a year," one visitor said, "are able to sit under the beginnings of their own vines and fig trees. Great pipelines are being laid from wells to the new farms. In many cases, water has to be conveyed over twenty miles under pressure for overhead irrigation of the croplands. Settlers and leaders alike are determined that their little country must become self-sufficient in food supplies and raw materials."

Greece. Across the Mediterranean, in this other ancient land of farming, the farmer's situation is almost as bad as it is in India. Wheat and corn yields average less than fifteen bushels to the acre . . . in contrast to many 100-bushel crops in the U.S.A. The typical Greek farm, including cropland, pasture, orchards, and grape vineyards, contains only nine acres. Few farmers can earn more than $250 per year, even though the women work with the men and ten-year-old children work every day in the tobacco fields or tend the flocks of sheep and goats. Greece, too, desperately needs more water and minerals for her soils, more forests, better seeds, and improved strains of livestock.

Poland. Two types of farms exist in this war-torn country on the shores of the North Sea. The country estates, once owned by the "landed gentry," vary from 150 to 1,000 acres. The workers on these farms were day laborers who had no opportunity for education. Since Poland became an ally of Soviet Russia at the end of World War II, most of these estates have been taken over by the government.

Other farms vary from fifty to ten acres. The smallest farms are called "dwarfs" and are made up of several parcels of land that may be a mile or two apart. The "dwarf" farmer lives in a village. His small potato field may be on the north side of town, his cow pasture on the south side, and his tiny grain field a mile east.

Polish farms, recent investigators report, are in dire need of more soil chemicals, better drainage, improved control of weeds and bugs, new types of machinery, and more sanitary barns.

Bolivia. On broad treeless plains among the Andes Mountains in South America, 12,000 feet above sea level, the descendants of America's first farmers grub a barren existence from worn-out soil.

Two types of farms exist in this Bolivian "altiplano," which is the Spanish word for "high plain." The large estates, known as "haciendas," are owned by wealthy families who live in the cities. A typical hacienda has 12,000 acres of land, and employs 150 Indian families. Each Indian family is permitted to cultivate from ten to twenty-five acres of land for its own use. In return, all members of the family must work three days a week for the hacienda. Cash wages are paid for additional work. They average twenty cents a day.

The second type of farm is called a "communidad" or "community farm." These are owned jointly by all the Indians in a village.

Frosts attack the crops during the growing season. The soil is poor in minerals and organic matter. The world's first potatoes were bred from wild plants in these mountains thousands of years ago. But potatoes grown there today are the size of English walnuts, and crops average twenty and thirty bushels to the acre (as compared to 400 bushels to the acre in Maine, New York State, Pennsylvania, and Idaho). More fertilizer, improved seed, and bug control would increase the altiplano's potato crop by 300 per cent in the opinion of experts who visited there in 1950.

Similar improvements can be made, these experts believe, in grain crops and livestock production through the use of some of the modern methods known to John Ferris and other American farmers.

We have visited only a few of the nations on the earth in our flying trip, yet the farming conditions we have found are typical of much of the world.

In Canada, our good neighbor to the north, farms are very much like those in the U.S.A., but the climate is colder and there are fewer cities. The first European

Australia is famous for its sheep farms

settlers in Canada were French. Ancient French traditions are still followed by farmers in eastern Canada. Work horses are big and strong. Farmhouses and barns are built of stone. These Canadian farmers produce some of the world's finest cheeses. The farm women are very skillful in spinning and weaving, and make excellent jams and jellies.

Western Canada is ranch country. The soil is deep black from the edge of the Ontario woodlands to the crest of the Rockies. These are the most famous wheatlands on the earth. But the winters are seven and eight months long. Airplanes, fitted with skis, are an important part of ranch equipment. Snowmobiles are becoming popular, too. These are large tractors with rubber tires eight feet high. The cabin where the rancher and his family ride is built of steel and heated by the engine. Snowmobiles can travel thirty miles an hour over snowdrifts twenty feet high.

Australia and New Zealand have large, fertile farms, too, where modern methods are used. Much of the interior of Australia, however, is desert country. It, too, needs water and minerals. The farms of Australia grow more sheep than any other country. They also produce big crops of wheat, oats, barley, corn, hay, potatoes, sugar cane, grapes, and fruit.

The Scandinavian countries and Great Britain, although their farms are small, have large farmer co-operatives. Rural living conditions are not so very different from our own.

Little is actually known about the farming conditions inside Soviet Russia in recent years, except that all land belongs to the government. Therefore farmers do not have the atmosphere of freedom we have in the free countries. We do know that co-operatives in Russia are "bossed" by the government, and that farmers have little say about running them. Taxes are higher too.

All of the facts we learned in our imaginary trip around the world have been discovered during the past few years by researchers for the F.A.O. of the United Nations. This is the most exciting, and hopeful, organization ever created for farmers. Its full name is the Food and Agricultural Organization. Its headquarters are in Rome, Italy. Many of its scientists and investigators come from the U.S.A.

The F.A.O. was founded on that ancient, but tried-and-true, farm idea of swapping. It was established by the United Nations in 1945 to enable farmers all over the world to swap helpful ideas with other farmers. In this way, John Ferris' system of spraying his apple trees can be most valuable to apple growers in Poland, and knowledge of the methods being used to develop farmland in Israel will be of great help to the farmers of India.

Dr. Raymond W. Miller, an experienced farmer from Linden, California is one of the investigators for F.A.O. Dr. Miller returned to the U.S.A. from a farm research trip around the world in the spring of 1951. This is what he said, when he got back home:

"This trip around the world served to confirm my strong belief that most of the world's problems are rural, and that they center around the desire of rural people—farmers, fishermen, and foresters—to live as other men. Agricultural reform holds the key, and self-help is the door. The people of all lands are basically like ourselves. God made us all. It happens that we have a head start in obtaining many of the material things of life. The American farming system, involving as it does self-help through co-operatives, credit facilities, and family ownership, coupled with extension work and farm research, makes for a sound rural economy and a good life for rural people. The system cannot be copied in full everywhere. But it can be studied, and parts can be used in other lands as they are needed.

"Eighty-five per cent of the people of the Far East live in

rural areas. The people of Asia are looking to the West to lend them the helping hand of friendship, and to provide them with technical advice and assistance. These people would like to be our neighbors, in the fullest sense of the word. And it would be mutually beneficial. The East has much to offer us in return for whatever assistance we may give. The real answer to most of the world's problems lies in assisting the rural peoples of the earth to attain a better standard of living."

And there, it seems to me, is an excellent place to end this story of the farm, for now we have the challenge of its future. Civilization was born on the farm. The crops that come from the soil are, and always will be, the power and fuel that enable civilization to continue. Farm improvement, therefore, means improvement for civilization—in cities and towns—on the land itself—everywhere.

So there is a great tomorrow for John and Margaret Ferris, for Big Dave Putnam, for the tractor makers, the fertilizer makers, the soil scientists, the thousands of researchers in photosynthesis and crop and livestock improvement. The big challenge of new pioneering days looms ahead for Betsy and David and Peggy. And for you, too.

FARM WORDS TO REMEMBER

Some of the words and phrases used in this book may be strange to you, especially if you happen to live in the city. So I have arranged most of the farm words used here into a dictionary for your use.

ACRE   An exact area of land, totaling 43,560 square feet or 4,840 square yards. The word is Anglo-Saxon in origin and originally meant "A tilled or enclosed field."

ANNUAL   Any plant that sprouts from seed in the spring, bears its crop the same summer, and dies in the fall.

APIARY   The Latin word for "bee" is "apis," so an apiary is a collection of beehives, *or* anywhere else that colonies of bees live. Wild bees make their own apiaries in old tree trunks.

APPLE   One of the oldest fruits in the world, so common in ancient Europe that early translators of the Bible gave its name to the fruit Eve ate. It is the round edible fruit of a type of tree called "malus" by the scientists. The Anglo-Saxons gave it its present name but spelled it "aeppel."

ARBOR   This is the old Latin word for "tree" or "beam of

wood." It has come to mean "an orchard" or a kind of latticework covered with vines or shade trees. Arbor Day, first observed in Nebraska, is a day in late April or May, set aside as a state holiday on which to plant more trees.

BACTERIA Forms of life so small that they can be seen only with strong microscopes. Soil bacteria turn fertilizers into foods that the plants can use for photosynthesis.

BARN This word has a very interesting history. It was compounded from two Anglo-Saxon words meaning "A closed place to store barley." Now it is the term for any large farm building where grains, hay, and feed are stored and where livestock, especially cows and horses, have their stables. A common type of American barn is the "bank barn," invented by the Pennsylvania Dutch 300 years ago.

BARNYARD A yard belonging to, and adjoining, a barn. It often has a wall or fence around it so that cows and horses can be let out in it to get exercise and sunlight during the winter months.

BEEVES The plural of "beef" and a word used by Western cattlemen in referring to a herd of beef cows. Some of the varieties of beef cow are: Hereford, Aberdeen Angus, Brahman, Shorthorns, Longhorns, Santa Gertrudis.

BIENNIAL A kind of plant that puts out roots and leaves the first year it is planted, but does not bear its fruit or seed until the second year. Sweet clover is a biennial.

BIN A big box where animal feeds and grains are stored.

BINDER A large machine that cuts hay, grain, or corn, then "binds," or ties it into bundles farmers can handle as a "package."

BLIGHT A kind of disease that causes plants to turn black or "spotty," and die.

BOAR The male of any breed of pig.

BOTTOM   This word, as used on most U.S.A. farms, refers to the flat, rich land lying in valleys beside rivers and lakes. Spring floods cover it, depositing silt and minerals. Hence this land is usually richer than the average, but at the expense of eroded hillsides "up the valley."

BUD   The cone-shaped swellings along the branches of plants and trees that contain the young shoots and flowers. Trees grow buds in the fall. These swell, burst open and let out the leaves or flowers in the spring.

BULB   The enlarged roots of onions, tulips, lilies, and other plants of the "alium" or "lilium" families.

BULL   The male of any breed of the genus, *Bos*, as scientists call the cow family.

BUSHEL   A standard of dry measure, used most commonly on the farm. One bushel equals four pecks or thirty-two quarts.

CALF   The young of most large animals, such as moose, elephants, whales, cows are called "calves." A "calf," on the farm, means a "young cow," under six months of age.

CELLAR   A room or set of rooms below the surface of the ground, used on the farm to store provisions for the farm family. On the prairies, many farms have "storm cellars" that are used as a place of refuge during cyclones.

CHICK   A young chicken or a young bird.

CHICKEN   This is the Anglo-Saxon name for the large birds tamed and bred thousands of years ago for fighting qualities as well as for their meat and eggs. Most breeds, such as Leghorn, Plymouth Rock, Rhode Island Red, etc. originated in India, China, or the East Indies.

CHLOROPHYLL   The green coloring matter of plants that processes the carbon dioxide we breathe out. With the help of sun power, the soil chemicals, and water, chlorophyll turns our stale air into the fresh oxygen we breathe in. It makes raw food for the plant from the carbon left over.

COLD FRAME A pit in the ground, with concrete or wooden sides and a window frame cover. The bottom of the pit is covered with cow manure and other fertilizers. Rich soil is poured atop this. Seeds like tomatoes, asters, broccoli, pepper, etc. are planted here. The window glass and manure keep the soil warm during frosty nights of early spring. When the plants are several inches high, they are transplanted into the garden.

COLT A young horse.

COMBINE A large machine that harvests and threshes grain while moving over the field.

COMPOST See Mulch.

CONSERVATION FOUNDATION This independent organization was founded in 1948 to investigate our soils, water supplies, forests and wildlife and to interest Americans in future conservation of these natural resources. The Foundation's headquarters is at 30 East 40th Street, New York City. Your school or club can obtain moving pictures about natural resources from the Conservation Foundation, as well as books and pamphlets.

COOLER A large tank, containing about two feet of cold water. Cow's milk is stored overnight in large cans in coolers kept near the barn. This keeps it fresh for morning delivery to the pasteurization plant in the village.

COOP The old farm term for the small house and wired enclosure where chickens are kept. Since chicken raising has become a more specialized business, the word has been pretty much discarded for terms like "henhouse," "chicken run," etc.

CO-OP "Co-op" is the slang term generally used on the

farm for "co-operative." A co-operative is a business owned and operated by its customers. There are two kinds. A "producer co-op" sells raw products from the land, such as apples, cattle, sheep, grain, etc. in wholesale lots. A "consumer co-op" purchases manufactured products such as clothing, feed, machines, steel in wholesale lots, then divides the purchases among its member-owners. Any information you want about farmers' co-operatives can be obtained from the National Council for Farmers Co-operatives at: 744 Jackson Place, Washington, D. C.

CORN This word was the common name for all kinds of grain in Europe. It means wheat in England, and oats in Scotland. When white settlers came to America they applied it to the big, strange grain that had been developed by the Indians. The Indians called this plant and its hard, yellow and white kernels, "maize." But the Pilgrims and the Spanish and French immigrants renamed it corn.

CORNCRIB This was an Indian invention. It used to be a small house built with wooden slabs. Ears of corn were stored in it during the winter months. The big trouble with wooden corncribs was that rats and mice could get in, and often stole most of the grain. Now corncribs are built of steel or aluminum, with small air holes punched in the walls. The rats and mice can't get in.

COUNTY AGENT An official appointed by the Extension Service of the U. S. Department of Agriculture to advise farmers and help them in their common problems. An agent is appointed for each farming county in the U.S.A. He usually has his headquarters in the county courthouse.

COW The adult female of any animal of the genus, *Bos*. (This is where the word "bossy" comes from.) There are "beef cows" (beeves) and "milk cows" (milkers). The word "cows" is used, carelessly, to indicate whole herds of the animals, including males, females, and calves.

COWBOY Anybody who herds cattle or even drives them home from pasture is a "cowboy." But the word has become associated with the range riders on the big cattle ranches of the prairies and the Far West.

COVER Crops such as alfalfa and legumes, grown on alternate years in fields used to raise corn, wheat, and the like. The "cover" crop feeds the soil with chemicals, and makes it possible to grow a better grain crop the following year.

CULTIVATOR A platform holding curved, steel teeth that look like small plows. Drawn across fields, this machine "cultivates" the soil by breaking up the clumps of dirt and tearing out weeds.

CURRYCOMB A brush with metal teeth, used to clean the fur of cows, horses, and sometimes pigs. "Curry" is from an ancient French word that means to "brush down" or "prepare."

DAIRY The department of a farm where milk cows are kept, and where milk is produced for sale or for processing into cream, butter, or cheese.

DISK A plow-like machine made of round, steel blades set at angles. It is drawn across a field to chop and pulverize the soil.

DRAG A general term for a machine used to break up clods of soil and level it, after plowing. A "disk" is one kind of a "drag." Another name for this type of machine is, "harrow."

DRILL A machine that makes holes or small furrows in a field, drops seeds and fertilizer into them and covers them.

ENSILAGE Livestock food, such as corn, alfalfa, green oats, that is chopped up raw, then blown into a silo to be used as year-round food for cattle, chickens, etc.

EROSION   The most dangerous evil of the farm. It is the process of soil being washed away from fields and hillsides, by heavy rains and floods, because of an absence of trees or cover crops.

F.A.O.   This is the organization set up by the United Nations to investigate farming conditions in every country on the earth, to find new methods for improving crops as well as farm life. The initials mean "Food and Agricultural Organization." Its world headquarters are in Rome, Italy. The head offices for the U.S.A. are at 1201 Connecticut Avenue N. W., Washington 6, D. C.

FARM BUREAU   This is a club and business organization for farm families. The Farm Bureau has offices and club-rooms in each county. Every state has a State Farm Bureau in the capital city. The national organization is called the American Farm Bureau Federation. It has headquarters in Chicago, Illinois, and Washington, D. C. The Farm Bureau is the strongest and most influential farm organization. It organized many of the farmers' co-operatives. Some of the State Farm Bureaus own oil wells, refineries, manufacturing plants, insurance companies and retail stores that sell products and services to their farmer-members at low prices.

FALLOW   Land that is plowed to destroy weeds and insects, then left to "mellow" for a year without replanting.

FARROW   A family of baby pigs.

FEED   Any mixture of chopped grains, grasses, fish oils, minerals, etc. used as a standard diet for farm animals.

FENCE   Any enclosure around a field. Rows of trees and stone walls were the original fences. Now barbed or meshed wire, strung on posts, are most commonly used.

FERTILIZER Any mineral or manure mixture worked into soil to enrich it.

FOAL Any young horse.

FORK A tool with two or more long, very sharp prongs, used to pick up small stacks of hay, straw and similar crops. Table forks are small imitations of farm forks.

FOUR-H Term used for clubs organized among farm boys and girls by the Extension Service of the State Colleges of Agriculture and the U. S. Dept. of Agriculture. Governmental agencies are aided, in their 4-H activities, by a volunteer organization: The National Committee on Boys and Girls Club Work, Inc., of Chicago. Boys and girls can join when they are ten. The four H's stand for: head, hands, heart, and health.

"FUTURE FARMERS" This is another organization for boys of high school age who are studying to be farmers. High schools with courses in "vocational agriculture" have Future Farmers of America clubs. The national organization is under the direction of the U. S. Office of Education in Washington, D. C.

GRANGE Founded in 1867, the Grange is the oldest American farm organization. It is actually a fraternity and has secret initiation rites. Its official name is the National Grange of the Patrons of Husbandry. Husbandry is the old word for farming. The Grange has chapters in most farming sections of the U.S.A. The head of each chapter is called the "Worthy Master." The Grange, like the Farm Bureau, organizes co-operatives and keeps a close watch on state and Federal government activities. Its national headquarters are in The Grange Building, 744 Jackson Place, N. W., Washington, D. C.

GREEN THUMB Some people have more skill, or luck,

than others in raising plants and flowers. A person who possesses this skill is said to "have a green thumb."

HAND   The slang term for a "hired man." Any person who works on the farm for day or monthly wages is known as a "hand."

HARDPAN   Layers of soil, usually composed of hard clay or gravel, that are extremely hard to plow through and that don't have enough moisture to enable crops to grow.

HARROW   Another word for "cultivator." Its metal teeth level off plowed soil, and break up the dirt clods.

HARVEST   The yield of any crop. Because most crops in the U.S.A. ripen in the fall, this season is known as "harvesttime."

HAYMOW   The top floor of a barn where hay is stored.

HAY RIG   A flat, wide frame mounted in a wagon. It is used to carry hay, cornstalks, straw, and other grassy crops in from the fields.

HERD   Any collection or assembly of large animals, such as cattle, horses, mules.

HIRED MAN   A man who works for wages on a farm as a "hand."

HORSE   The large, four-footed work animal descended from the family scientists call "Equus caballus." It has been largely replaced by the tractor on farms in the U.S.A.

HYBRID   The seed, or offspring, coming from the union of a male of one variety, species or race and the female of another. Most of the corn grown in the U.S.A. today is "hybrid." A mule is a hybrid. For that matter, so are most Americans.

INCUBATION   The process of hatching eggs into baby fowl, either through the use of an "incubator" machine or through warmth from the mother.

INSECTICIDE Any spray, dust or gas used to kill bugs and insects that damage crops.

LAND-GRANT COLLEGES As the West was settled, and the Indians were defeated, the Federal Government took over all the land. Later, the western states were organized. After 1862, by Act of Congress, thousands of acres of Federal land in each new state were turned over to the state, with the understanding that all profits made from the sale, or use of, the land would go toward the support of schools-of-agriculture. This was the beginning of most of the State Colleges of Agriculture. These colleges are still called the "Land-Grant Colleges."

LIME A powder obtained by grinding limestone, seashells, or other forms of calcium carbonate. Lime is spread on fields to "sweeten" the soil and produce larger crops. The Indians broke up seashells and spread them in their crop fields. They used dead fish for fertilizer, too.

LIVESTOCK All animals raised by the farmer for profit.

MANURE SPREADER This is a very tricky machine invented 100 years ago by a country schoolteacher at Coldwater, Ohio. A manure spreader looks like a box wagon except for the rows of steel pedals fixed into a drum at the rear. And the bottom of the wagon is a moving belt. Both the belt and the steel pedals are geared to the wheels. When the manure spreader is pulled across a field, the belt moves the load of manure toward the rear, the pedals kick it off, and spread it evenly across the field.

MARKET The place in the town or city where the farmer sells his crops.

MEADOW A field on which grass is grown for hay, or for grazing by livestock.

MILK The whitish fluid obtained from the mammary

glands of all female mammals, but most commonly obtained on the farm from cows. Butter, cheese, clothing, paint, writing paper, and even hats are made from it.

MILKER   The slang word for the machine that milks cows.

MILKING MACHINE   A machine with rubber cups that fit over the teats of a milk cow's udder. Air suction, created by an electric motor, pulls out the milk. A milking machine will milk a cow in five minutes. Hand milking takes nine minutes per cow.

MOW   (Pronounced "moe.") The process of cutting grass or grain; (Pronounced "maoww") a slang term for "hay-mow."

MULCH   Leaves, straw, grass, sawdust, or other materials spread on shrubs and perennials to protect them from the alternating freezing and thawing of the winter months. Old mulch, mixed with lime and minerals, rots down and becomes an excellent, rich soil fertilizer called "compost."

NEIGHBOR   This is another farm word. It originally meant "near by farmer," but now applies to any family or person living in the vicinity of your home.

ORCHARD   Any group of trees planted for crops, such as nuts, fruit, or sap (i.e., turpentine, maple sugar) etc.

PASTURE   A field set aside for grazing by livestock.

PECK   A quarter of a bushel; eight quarts.

PEN   A small yard for animals, usually made of wooden slats or wire mesh and placed either indoors or outdoors.

PERENNIAL   Any plant that will live out of doors through the winter and grow from one year to another. All trees are perennials. So are roses, lilies, tulips, and grasses.

PHOTOSYNTHESIS   The still unknown process by which sunlight creates chlorophyll, causes it to break down the air we breathe out and then transform it into growing plants and fresh air.

PIG   Any of the species of swine.

PLOW (PLOUGH)   Any machine used to cut into, turn over, and break up soil.

PONY   A horse of any small, but stocky, breed. It is noted for its patience and sturdiness. The ponies of the Shetland Islands and Iceland are best known.

PORKER   A term for "pig" derived from "porcus," the Latin word for "pig."

POWER TAKE-OFF   A gear shaft built into the side of most tractors. Wheels can be attached to it to run saws, choppers and other machines via a belt drive. Before power take-offs were installed on tractors, farmers jacked up the rear ends of old cars, and powered their machines from the spinning wheels.

PRUNE   (a) Trim off the dead, or excess, wood on a tree, bush or vine. Fruit trees, left unpruned, will use most of their energy to grow branches. Hence, the fruit will be small. (b) A variety of dried plum.

PULLET   A young hen, less than a year old.

RAM   A male sheep.

RANCH   This comes from the Spanish word "rancho" meaning "a place where herdsmen live." It now applies to any farm in the Far West. There are orange ranches of not more than five acres in California. But, of course, most of us think of a "ranch" as a big prairie or mountain farm in the West where beef cattle and horses are raised.

REAP   The harvesting of any crop.

REAPER   Any machine for harvesting grain, or any person so engaged.

ROOSTER   Any male chicken.

ROTARY A type of plow with rapidly revolving blades that prepares the field for planting in a single operation.

ROTATION The system of planting crops so that soils will not lose all their minerals. Planting of corn, alfalfa, or oats in a field on successive years is a familiar type of "rotation."

SEED The tiny packets, pouches, or pellets grown in the fall by most plants for the purpose of producing their offspring, or "babies." Each seed contains a "life" that will make it grow to be like its parents. The seed also contains a food supply and a shell to help it get through the winter. Plants use all sorts of tricks to spread their seeds across the Earth. Maple seed has propellerlike wings so that the wind will carry it a long distance. Seeds like cockleburs have hooks and barbs in them that snag clothing or the fur of animals to "give them a lift" to new growing places.

SHARECROPPER A farmer who operates land to get a "share" of the crop, but doesn't own the land. The term is used most in the South, where the practice developed on cotton and rice plantations.

SHEEP The four-legged animal of the genus "ovis" that provides wool. Its flesh is eaten as "lamb" or "mutton." The skin produces soft leather. Parchment paper was originally made from sheepskins.

SHOOT The stem of a plant with its leaves.

SILO A round, tall and hollow building of wood, concrete, tile, or steel used for the storage of ensilage.

SOW (a) An adult female pig.

SOW (b) The process of planting seed.

SPRINGHOUSE Milk must be kept cool until it is delivered to the creamery. Before the days of electric refrigeration, dairy farmers piped water from a spring down to the trough where the cans of fresh milk were stored. The trough was usually in a small outbuilding adjoining the barn. This was nicknamed the "springhouse." The nickname still stands, although now most milk is cooled by electrical refrigeration.

SPROUT   The first spring growths that come out of seeds or tree trunks.

STALLS   The compartments in barns where horses or cows are kept. "Box stalls" are enclosed, small rooms where spirited or dangerous animals, such as bulls, are tied.

STANCHIONS   Upright bars, with drop-locks, that fit loosely around animal's necks and hold them still. They are used mostly on cows during milking time.

TENANT   A farmer who lives on and operates a farm but doesn't own the land.

THRESHER   A machine that beats out (i.e. threshes) grain from the stalks; any person who operates such a machine.

TOOLROOM   The building, or room, where machines and big tools such as the welder are stored, and where farm machines are repaired.

TOPSOIL   The top layer of soil on the surface of the earth. It has much plant and animal refuse and minerals in it and therefore produces the best crops. Topsoil varies in thickness from six inches to fifteen feet.

TRACTOR   A farm machine used for hauling and field work. It has four wheels and an engine like an automobile, but only one seat which is for the driver. The front wheels are smaller than an auto's. The rear wheels are four or five feet high, and sometimes have steel cleats instead of tires. Some tractors have caterpillar-treads.

U. S. D. A.   These are the initials of the United States Department of Agriculture, the branch of the U. S. Government that deals with Agriculture. Its headquarters are in two great buildings near the Washington Monument in Washington, D. C. It has over 80,000 employes, located in offices in every large city and every county seat. The Secretary of Agriculture and the Director of Extension Service are the two most important executives of U. S. D. A.

VEAL   The flesh of a calf, used for food.

VEGETATION   A common term for green, growing plants and trees.

WEANING   The process of changing the diet of a baby calf or other young animal from milk to solid foods.

WELDER   A kind of blow torch machine used to melt together pieces or parts of metal. There were over 2,000,000 welding machines on American farms in 1950. When machines break, farmers weld them back together again.

WOOD LOT   An area of the farm devoted to growing forest trees.

WOODSHED   A shed, built adjoining the farm kitchen, for the storage of firewood. This was essential when farmers burned only wood in their stoves and furnaces. Now most farmhouses have coal or gas heat, but the woodsheds remain, and are used for all kinds of storage.

YARD   A small enclosed place around a house, barn, or other building.

INDEX

Rotary, 184
Rotation, 184

Salt pork, 117
Sand, 147
Sausage, 117
Scandinavia, 169
School bus, 50–51
Seed, 11, 29, 33, 61, 71, 76, 184
"Set," 31
Sharecropper, 184
Sheep, 38-39, 139, 143, 184
Shoot, 184
Siam, 164
Silage, 92
Silo, 91, 94, 184
Skunk, 28–29
Smudge pots, 137
Snowmobiles, 168
Soil, 25, 43–44, 144, 146
Soil Conservation Service, 52
Soviet Russia, 169
Sow, 184
Specialty crops, 35
Spraying, 92
Spring, 43, 61, 99
Springhouse, 184
Sprout, 185
Stalls, 185
Stanchion, 185
Steer, 124
Sugar cane, 25, 137, 164
Summer, 30, 43
Sun, 28, 30, 43, 46, 72, 80, 144, 146, 154–155
Swift, Gustavus, 23

Tangerine, 25
Tank car, 39
Temperature, 28, 60

Tenant, 185
Thailand, 164
Thresher, 185
Tobacco, 16, 135
Toolroom, 185
Topsoil, 185
Trace elements, 149
Tractor, 26, 43, 54, 56, 185
Traders, 14
Trees, 97–98
Trench silo, 94
Truck, 26, 34, 39, 56, 88
Tung, 35, 138

Upland cotton, 41
U. S. Department of Agriculture, 24, 48, 132, 185

Veal, 186
Vegetation, 186

Wagon, 13
Washington, George, 20, 58
Water, 145, 153, 155
Weaning, 186
Webster, Daniel, 9, 15
Weeds, 61, 97
Welder, 186
Welding machine, 100
Wheat, 23, 41, 139
Wheel, 13, 25–26, 183
Whitney, Eli, 21, 40, 161
Winter, 30, 43, 99
Wood, Jethro, 21
Wood lot, 186
Woodshed, 186

Yard, 186
Yearling, 124
Young Farmers clubs, 122

191